DESIGN D&T MAKE IT !

Boo ... be returned on or before

textiles
technology
revised edition

WITHDRAWN

Alex McArthur ■ Carolyn Etchells ■ Tristram Shepard

Nelson Thornes
a Wolters Kluwer business

First published in 1997 by:
Stanley Thornes (Publishers) Ltd

Second edition published in 2001 by:
Nelson Thornes Ltd
Delta Place
27 Bath Road
CHELTENHAM
GL53 7TH
United Kingdom

07 / 10 9 8 7 6

A catalogue record for this book is available from the British Library

ISBN 978 0 7487 6082 4

Designed by Carla Turchini
Illustrations by Andrew Loft, Hardlines, Mark Dunn, John Fowler
and Tristram Ariss
Picture research by Jennie Karrach and johnbaily@axonimages.com
Printed and bound in China by Midas Printing International Ltd

The authors would particularly like to thank the following for their
contribution:
Lynn Beech, Anna Roberts, Brian Dickie of Skopos, Roy Jarratt, Ruth
Rundle and Pauline Treuherz; also Mark Hall, Tracy Leeson and Emma
Rough of Minster College, Sheppey, Kent for modelling the project
outcomes.

Contents

Project Three: A Sea Cruise

Project Suggestions

Introduction

Welcome to Design & Make It: Textiles Technology. *This book has has been written to support you as you work through your GCSE course in Design and Technology. It will help guide you through the important stages of your coursework, and assist your preparation for the final examination paper.*

Long or short?

If you are following a short course, check with your teacher which sections of the book you do not need to cover.

Making it

Whatever your project, remember that the final realisation is particularly important. It is not enough just to hand in your design folder. You must have separate textile products which you have made. The quality of your final realisation must be as high as possible as it counts for a high proportion of the marks.

During your course you will need to develop technical skills in using fabrics and equipment. This is something you can't do just by reading a book! The best way is to watch carefully as different techniques and procedures are demonstrated to you, and practise them as often as possible.

IN YOUR PROJECT

Special 'In Your Project' paragraphs help you to think about how you could apply the content of the pages to your current work.

How to Use this Book

There are two main ways the book might be used.

1   Follow the three design and make projects in sequence over the whole course, including a selection of the suggested activities (i.e. focused practical tasks). This will ensure complete syllabus coverage. You may decide not to take all of them as far as the production of a finished working product.

2   Undertake alternative projects to one or more of those provided and refer to those pages which cover the specific areas of knowledge and understanding defined in the examination syllabus and the KS4 National Curriculum.

Contents

Project guide

The book begins with a coursework guide which summarises the design skills you will need for extended project work. Refer back to these pages throughout the course.

The projects

Three projects are then provided. These each contain a mixture of product analysis and development pages and knowledge and understanding pages (e.g. Embellishment, Fibres and Fabrics) which include short focused tasks. In each of the projects the development of one possible solution has been used as an ongoing example. You could closely base your own work on this solution, but if you want to achieve higher marks you will need to try to come up with ideas of your own.

Project Suggestions

Finally two outline project suggestions are provided. Refer to the Project Guide to help develop your ideas and to ensure you are covering and documenting your coursework in the way the examiners will be looking for.

■ ACTIVITY

Make sure that as part of your design folder you include evidence of having completed a number of short-term focused practical tasks as suggested in the Activity sections.

KEY POINTS

Use the 'Key Points' paragraphs to revise from when preparing for the final examination paper. Three specimen papers are included at the end of the projects.

Beyond GCSE

Textiles and clothing production is one of the fastest growing industries in the world, and UK manufacturers now operate on a global scale.

There are good opportunities for skilled people to work in manufacturing. Another alternative is to train as a textile, fashion, theatre or interior designer, or in design management, marketing and retailing or textile technology. Such people need to be flexible, good communicators, willing to work in teams, and to be computer literate.

There are a wide range of further courses and training opportunities available at various levels which you might like to find out more about.

Design Matters

As you develop your ideas for textile products you will often need to make important decisions about the social, moral, cultural and environmental impact of your product.

Design and Technology is about improving people's lives by designing and making the things they need and want. But different people have different needs: what is beneficial to one person can cause a problem for someone else, or create undesirable damage to the environment.

Textile Products are manufactured within a social and cultural context which designers and manufacturers need to take into account. As well as needing to be aware of current fashion and style trends they should be aware of the effects that their activities and products have on people and the world around them.

Design for profit

Products are designed and made to make life easier and more enjoyable, or to make a task or activity more efficient. However, along the way the people who create these products need to make a profit. The designer needs to do more than satisfy the needs of the market, and to consider the sorts of issues described on the next page. They must also take into account the needs of the clients, manufacturers and retailers. The aim is to design and make products that are successful from everyone's point of view.

A brief history of textiles technology

Weaving is one of the oldest crafts. A fine linen shirt preserved in the tomb of Tutenkhamun dates from around 1360 BC. Such survivals are extremely rare and evidence of early textiles mostly exists in visual evidence such as the depiction of fine garments on Pompeiian wall paintings.

A Pompeiian wall painting

Everyday cloth was produced locally but an international market in luxury textiles developed. The movement of textiles within Europe was extensive and trade even reached to the Far East. During the first century BC, Chinese textiles brought by camel caravans reached the Mediterranean.

Social issues

Many textile and clothing companies have their goods produced abroad because labour costs are cheaper which means they can sell the products at a more competitive price. However, the local workforce is often exploited and some companies have used child labour. Are you happy to buy a product knowing that it has been made in this way?

Cultural awareness

People from different cultures think and behave in different ways. What is acceptable to one culture may be confusing or insulting to another. Fabric colours, patterns and images can have very different meanings across the world.

Moral issues

Public pressure has been used to dissuade cosmetics companies from testing their products on animals and to dissuade designers against breeding animals to make garments from fur.

Environmental issues

We all need to be aware of the amount and use of energy and resources, as on our earth these are finite. The more we use up natural resources without replacing them, the fewer there are for future generations.

Textile manufacturers use vast stretches of land to produce cotton and they use pesticides to make crop yields as profitable as possible.

A new solution to this problem is the use of biotechnology research to improve pest and disease resistance of the cotton plant and to increase its tolerance towards herbicides. Long term aims are to bio-modify the processing and end-use performance characteristics of the cotton fibre. However, will the fury over GM food crops turn to GM cotton crops? What will the impact be on retailers who are currently unable to identify whether a fabric uses GM cotton or not?

During the Medieval period natural dyes were used and the four natural fibres of wool, linen, cotton and silk. Fabrics were usually left plain or dyed a single colour. For more luxurious fabrics decoration was applied in the weave either by tapestry or the drawloom, by embroidery or more rarely by simple printing methods.

Between 1550 and 1780 the wool, linen and silk industries developed in response to an expanding market within Europe and in new territories such as the Americas. Trade with India and China opened up and they provided not only raw material like silk and cotton but also finished goods including Indian painted and printed cottons known as 'chintzes'.

Industrial Matters

Good design involves creating something that works well and is satisfying to use. But to be successful a product also needs to be commercially viable.

Choice and change

Today people can chose from a huge variety of fashion, accessories and soft furnishings products to enhance their daily lives. Regarding clothing as a commercial commodity rather than a necessity has seen the development of a global textile industry.

Changes in society bring constantly changing needs and demands which manufacturing industry strives to meet. Manufacturers need to constantly develop new technological advances in fabrics in order to give them an advantage over their competitors.

Market research

Designers and manufacturers use market research to try and determine what it is that consumers really want. They must be aware of demographic changes in the population and they must target and research the needs of a particular consumer group in order to launch the right product at the right price for them onto the market.

For example, baby boomers and the ageing population will create significant new markets over the next few years, in terms of both demographics and spending power. By the year 2010 people over the age of 55 will become the largest consumer group in the UK. It has become clear that clothing manufacturers and retailers will have to adapt their product offerings to cater for the need of this age group if they are to attain any significant market growth in the future.

New high-tech textiles and clothing companies are already tapping into these needs. For example, shirts that can monitor the health of the wearer, recording vital signs such as heart rate and breathing are being developed. This information can then be downloaded through the internet and assessed by qualified staff.

The eighteenth century was a great period of technical innovation in the textiles industry. Most manufacturing processes were mechanised, speeding up production, increasing the range of available products and reducing labour costs. This aroused hostility among workers who saw it as a threat to their employment.

By the 1850s the replacement of natural dyes with synthetics was well underway. This was a result of the use of aniline dyestuffs, based on benzine oil which was extracted from coal tar and combined with acid to achieve colour. The sewing machine for domestic and small scale manufacture was introduced during the 1850s.

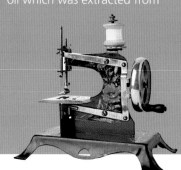

Case Study: Lycra

Throughout the history of textiles new fibres and technologies have provided us with fabrics of different properties. Since the advent of synthetic fibres in the 1950s and 1960s many have passed by and become known only as a fashion fad.

Lycra first arrived in the UK in the late 1950s and many in industry were unaware of the impact it would have on World fashion 40 years later. With its unique ability to stretch, yet remain undetected, Lycra has brought possibilities of feel, form and fit previously only dreamt of by designers and manufacturers. Today it is found in a wide variety of fabrics from mixtures of cotton and silk to suiting fabrics, jeans and corduroy.

Lycra's launch coincided with the swinging 60s, a period of emancipation for women and increasing demand for more versatile fabrics and forms of clothing. In the body conscious 80s Lycra was the natural choice for leggings. Today designers have explored the possibility of mixing lycra with the more fluid styles and the range of fabrics containing a small percentage of elastane has increased to include denim, linen and the finest crepe de chine.

Lycra can be sheathed with another yarn or fibre so that it adopts the characteristics of the fibre it is mixed with. These yarns can then be combined during weaving or knitting with non-elastic yarns.

Case Study: Teflon Fibre

Consumers have until recently identified Teflon with non-stick cooking utensils but it is now also produced in fibre form, where it provides a striking example of the effect of structure on performance. The majority of its applications have been in high performance technical textiles but now it is also used for clothing. Teflon has long been used to make high-performance sewing threads, for use in hot-gas filtration equipment and other textiles where good flex, strength, heat and chemical-resistance are required. It is also used in medical textiles and, more recently, as the low rub ingredient in friction-resistant clothing. In sports socks sections with Teflon fibres help avoid the formation of blisters.

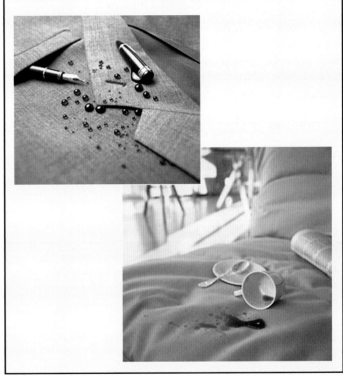

In recent years CAD-CAM has transformed the textiles industry. There have been amazing developments in materials technology, providing fabrics with extraordinary characteristics and properties. While many of these will radically change our fabrics and garments, some may never be more than novelty items. How long do you think there will be a demand for scented underwear and thermal regulating garments?

A fabric woven from nylon and lycra at high magnification.

Clothes can include recycled plastic in the fabric.

ICT in the Textiles Industry

The use of ICT (Information and Communication Technology) has had a major impact on the textiles industry during the past 20 years.

 Using the Internet

Using the internet, textile companies can now receive information and daily industry news 24 hours a day from around the world. All this information is used in different ways, depending on the particular market the company operates in.

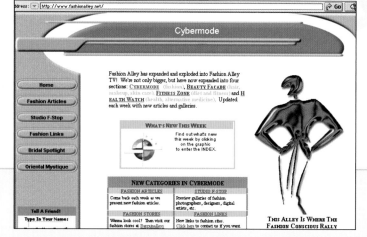

Trade Show Reports – from major international shows, showing pictures of new designs and images.

Catwalks – full collections, analysis and overviews.

Trend Forecasting – for women's, men's, kids, active sport , youth, underwear, footwear, home and interiors.

Trend Tracking – this follows the developments in styling, colour and textiles, across the world in major cities.

Consumer Research – looking at what the consumer is spending money on from LA, New York, London Paris, Milan and Tokyo.

Market Data – what's hot, what's not, what are the latest things on the street.

Visual Merchandising – many stores use images of their window displays as a way of promoting designers and events.

Guides, Maps and Listings – showing the best places to shop for fabrics, etc.

Sourcing Resources – information about companies that provide a wide range of goods and services, and on-line ordering of samples/fabrics, etc.

New Talent – Graduate Portfolios of the latest and newest designers at leading fashion colleges.

Financial Information – company results, stock market movements, analyst summaries, etc.

CAD-CAM

One of the main uses of ICT in the textiles industry is for CAD-CAM (Computer Aided Design and Computer Aided Manufacture). CAD is a system for creating, modifying and communicating ideas for a product or components of a product. CAM is when manufacturing processes are carried out aided by a computer. These may include process control, planning, monitoring and controlling production.

CAD-CAM has a number of significant advantages:

▷ Drawings or designs can be scanned into the computer and a wide range of repeat patterns and colour options generated in minutes.

▷ Chosen designs can be textured with different fabric types to show what the fabric can look like. Finished designs can then be 'draped' or image mapped onto a model, or furniture, an interior, and can then be shown in a variety of styles, etc.

▷ The finished fabrics can be chosen from the screen by the client and then printed using a digital printer. All the details can be used for production printing.

▷ Data from pattern-making programs can be used to instruct machines to cut the pieces out from lengths of fabric

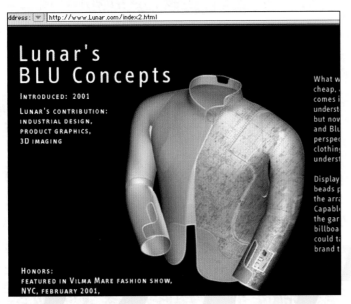

Lunar's
BLU Concepts

INTRODUCED: 2001

LUNAR'S CONTRIBUTION:
INDUSTRIAL DESIGN,
PRODUCT GRAPHICS,
3D IMAGING

HONORS:
FEATURED IN VILMA MARE FASHION SHOW,
NYC, FEBRUARY 2001,

The garment shown above would be able to display images and text directly on the fabric. The material is composed of a matrix of microscopic beads. These pick up radio transmissions that control the colour and brightness of each bead. You could use it to find your way around, watch TV on, or as a moving advertisement!

Yesterday, today and tomorrow

The use of ICT as a tool in all areas of the textile industry has grown considerably. Ten years ago ICT was used mainly used in the following areas:

▷ pattern cutting and marker-making
▷ pattern grading
▷ costing

Today ICT is also used in the following ways:

▷ as a design tool – designing products, such as fabrics, motifs
▷ as a manufacturing / production tool
▷ as a communication tool
▷ as a sales tool

In the future it is predicted that ICT will be widely used for:

▷ digital printing – direct to fabric
▷ 3D modelling – being able to model ideas and designs in 3D
▷ body scanning – as a method of creating customised designs
▷ creating virtual products in virtual environments
▷ garments and textile products that incorporate computer technology.

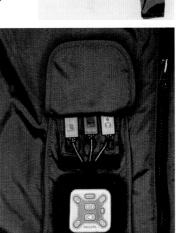

Wired garments

KEY POINTS

The main impact of ICT on the textile industry has been:
● many tasks, especially repetitive ones, can be done much more quickly and cheaply
● the more rapid global exchange of data and product information
● more sophisticated modelling of ideas and concepts leading to more creative designs
● the means by which to respond to market changes much more quickly
● the development of new synthetic fibres and fabrics with unique properties and characteristics

Using ICT in GCSE Textiles Technology

ICT (Information and Communication technology) is widely used in the design and production of products, as you will discover. You can considerably enhance your GCSE coursework with the effective use of ICT.

 ## Using ICT in your work

To gain credit for using ICT you need to know when it is best to use a computer to help with your work. Sometimes it is easier to use ICT to help with parts of your coursework than to do it another way. On other occasions it can be far easier to write some notes on a piece of paper than use a computer – this saves you time and helps you to do the job more effectively.

Following are some ideas showing you how using ICT could enhance your coursework. Some can be used at more than one stage. You do not have to use all them!

Identifying the Problem

The **internet** could be used to search manufacturers' and retailers' web-sites for new products, indicating new product trends.

Project Planning

A time chart can be produced showing the duration of the project and what you hope to achieve at each stage using a **word processor** or **DTP** program. Some programs allow you to produce a Gantt chart (See page 125).

Investigation

▷ A questionnaire can be produced using a **word processor** or **DTP**. Results from a survey can be presented using a **spreadsheet** as a variety of graphs and charts.

▷ Use a **digital camera** to record visits and existing products

▷ The **internet** can be used to perform literature searches and communicate with other people around the world via **e-mail**.

Search engines

To help you find the information you need on the internet you can use a search engine. A search engine is a web-site that allows you to type in keywords for a specific subject. It then scans the internet for web sites that match what you are looking for. Here are the addresses of some popular search engines:

www.excite.co.uk
www.yahoo.co.uk
www.netscape.com
www.hotbot.co.uk
www.msn.co.uk
www.searchtheweb.com

E-mail

E-mail is a fast method of communicating with other people around the world. Text, photographs and computer files can be attached and shared. Some web-sites have e-mail addresses – you could try to contact experts to see if they could help with your coursework. It is important to be as specific as you possibly can, as these experts may be very busy people.

Specification

A design or product specification can be written in a **word processor**. Visual images of the product, diagrams and other illustrations could also be added. Information can be easily modified at a later date.

Developing ideas

▷ Ideas for your product could be produced using a **graphics** program, **DTP** or **3D CAD** package. Colour variations can be applied to product drawings to test a design on its intended market before production. You can use a variety of surface decoration techniques in order to improve the aesthetic qualities of textiles, fabrics and products; e.g. appliqué,, beading, collage, machine embroidery, You can use graphics software to design fabric, and experiment with techniques.

▷ The likely costs of new products can be modelled using a **spreadsheet**. Different component costs can be modelled quickly and easily allowing you to see the consequences of your design ideas.

▷ **CAD** and **CAM** can be used when you are designing logos and motifs that can be embroidered. CAD to design the motif and CAM (a prototype) on a **Computerised sewing machine**. CAD designs can be done using a graphics or paint program and saved for further development in the sewing machine software

▷ **CAD** and **CAM** can also be used when developing designs using a computerised knitting machine

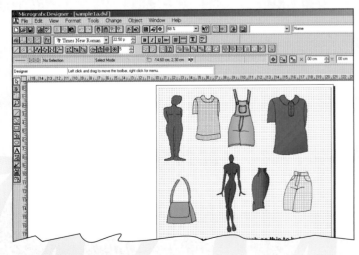

You can use programs such as this to help you plan ideas and colours.

Final Ideas and Production

▷ A document showing the specification, images, production method and components can be **word-processed**.

▷ Parts lists and the costs of materials can be calculated and displayed using **spreadsheets**.

▷ A detailed flow production diagram could be produced using a **DTP** program. Images could also be added to show important stages.

▷ **Digital images** can be used in the production plan as a guide to show how the product should be assembled or to indicate its colour.

▷ Pre-programmed **CAM** equipment could be used to replicate manufacture,

Project presentation

▷ Use **graphics** packages to prepare text and visual material for presentation panels. Charts showing numerical data can be quickly produced using a **spreadsheet**.

▷ Use a **presentation** package, such as *PowerPoint* to communicate the main features of your design.

ICT

Choosing and Starting Projects

Identifying suitable design and make projects for yourself is not easy. A carefully chosen project is much more likely to be interesting and easier to complete successfully. Investing time and effort choosing a good project makes progress a lot easier later on.

Project Feasibility Studies

Make a start by making a list of:

▷ potential local situations/environments you could visit where you could do some research into the sort of things people there might need (e.g. a local playgroup, a hospital or old people's home, etc.)

▷ people you know outside school who might be able to help by providing information, access and / or advice.

The next stage is to get up and get going. Arrange to visit some of the situations you've listed. Choose the ones which you would be interested in finding out some more about. Make initial contact with the people you know, and get them interested in helping you. Tell them about your D&T course, and your project.

You should visit each possible situation to identify people's needs and spot opportunities to help solve their problems with new textile products.

With a bit of luck, after you've done the above you should have a number of ideas about possible projects.

Try to identify what the possible outcomes of your projects might be – not what the final design would be, but the form your final realisation might take, e.g. a finished garment of printed fabric made into a product, a sample, series of text pieces, presentation artwork, etc. Think carefully about the following:

▷ Might it be expensive or difficult to make?

▷ Do you have access to the equipment and materials which would be required?

▷ Will you be able to find out how it could be printed or manufactured?

▷ Does the success of the project depend on important information you might not be able to get in the time available?

▷ Are there good opportunities for you to use ICT?

the home

energy

the natural environment

the high street

transport

communications

clothing

leisure

security

food

health

education

starting points

There are different ways in which you might be able to start a project. Your teacher may have:

● told you exactly what you are required to design

● given you a range of possible design tasks for you to choose from

● left it up to you to suggest a possible project.

If you have been given a specific task to complete you can go straight on to page 16.

If you are about to follow one of the main units in this book, you should go straight to the first page of the task.

If you have been given a number of possible tasks to choose from you should go straight to the section entitled 'Making your Choice'.

However, if you need to begin by making some decisions about which will be best task for you, then the first stage is to undertake some feasibility studies.

Making Your Choice

For each of your possible projects work through pages 16 and 17 (Project Investigation) and try planning out a programme of research.

Look back over your starting questions and sources of information:

▷ Could you only think up one or two areas for further research?
▷ Did you find it difficult identifying a range of sources of information?

If this has been the case, then maybe it is not going to prove to be a very worthwhile project.

Ideally, what you're looking for is a project which:

▷ is for a nearby situation you can easily use for research and testing
▷ you can get some good expert advice about
▷ provides good opportunities for you to do a range of research activities and an expected outcome which will make it possible for you to make and test a prototype
▷ will not be too difficult to finally realise
▷ shows a good use of ICT
▷ is suitable for manufacture.

Finally, one of the most important things is that you feel interested and enthusiastic about the project!

don't forget...

A very important consideration is the testing of a prototype of some sort, and of your final design. How would you be able to do this? Could ICT be used?

Remember that it's important that what you design is suitable for production, even if only in small numbers. It can't be a one-off item for you or a friend. You will need to show plans for your product to be reproduced or manufactured.

Don't forget to record all your thoughts and ideas about these initial stages of choosing and starting your project.

In your project folio provide a full record of the ideas you reject, and the reasons why. This helps provide important evidence of your decision-making skills, and of the originality of your project. Communication skills are important.

If you come up with more than one good idea, find out how many projects you have to submit at the end of your course. You might be able to do one or more of your other ideas at a later date.

Make sure you discuss your project ideas with a teacher.

in my design folder

✓ My project is to design a...
✓ I am particularly interested in...
✓ I have made a very good contact with...
✓ My prototype can be tested by...
✓ My final outcome will include...
✓ I could use ICT to...

Project Investigation

You will need to find out as much as you can about the people and the situation you are designing for. To do this you will need to identify a number of different sources of information to research into.

Starting Questions

Make a list of questions you will have to find answers to.

You should find the following prompts useful:

Why...?

When...?

Where...?

What...?

How many...?

How much...?

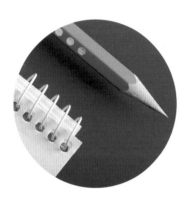

Sources of Information

Next, carefully consider and write down the potential sources of information you might be able to use in order to discover the answers to your starting questions.

Work through the research methods on the next page. Be sure to give specific answers as far as possible (i.e. name names).

Across your research you will need to aim to obtain overall a mixture of:

▷ factual information: e.g. size, shape, weight, cost, speed, etc.
▷ information which will be a matter of opinion: i.e. what people think and feel about things, their likes and dislikes, what they find important, pleasing, frustrating, etc.

don't forget...

Write down what you need to find out more about, and how you could obtain the information.

You need to use a range of sources of information (e.g. user research, existing solutions, expert opinion, information search). The more methods you use, the more marks you will get.

When you undertake the research, remember to record what you discover.

Make sure your research work is clearly and attractively presented.

in my design folder

✓ The key things I need to find out about are...
✓ The research methods I am going to use are...
✓ I will be talking to the following people about my project...
✓ I will need to have it all completed by...
✓ I will use ICT to...

Research Methods

User Research

Which people could you observe and consult who are directly involved in the situation? To what extent do you consider that you will be able to find out about:
- the things they do
- the way in which they do them.

As well as asking individuals, you could also undertake a small survey or questionnaire.

User Trips

How can you record your own impressions of the situation? Are there any relevant activities you could try out for yourself to gain first-hand experience? Do you have any recollections of any previous similar experiences you have had?

Site Study

In what ways could you document the environment in which the situation is? Which of the following will be relevant?
- Historical and geographical factors.
- Sociological, economic, political information.
- Location.
- Layout, facilities.
- Sizes and spaces.
- Atmosphere – light, colour, texture.
- The surrounding environment.

Similar Situations

Do you know of any other comparative circumstances in which people are in similar situations, and which might help provide insight and ideas?

Expert Opinion

Are there any people you know of who could give you expert professional advice on any aspects of the situation? If you don't know immediately of anyone, how might you set about finding somebody?

Information Search

Has any information about the situation, or a similar situation, been documented already in books, magazines, TV programmes, the internet, or CD-ROM, etc.? If you don't already know that such information exists, where could you go to look for it? Don't forget to consider the possibility of using information stored on a computer database.

In Conclusion

When most of your investigation work has been completed you will need to draw a series of conclusions from what you have discovered. What have you learnt about the following things:

▷ What sort of people are likely to be using the product?
▷ Where and when will they be using it?
▷ What particular features will it need to have?
▷ How many should be made?

Of all the research methods, user-research tends to be the most effective and useful, so you are highly recommended to include some in your investigation. Some form of personal contact is essential to a really successful project.

It is also highly advisable to conduct some form of questionnaire. If you have not done one to submit as part of your coursework, make sure that you will have the opportunity to do so this time.

It isn't necessary to use all the research methods in any one project, but you certainly must show that you have tried a selection of them.

in my design folder

✓ From my research I found out...
✓ keywords I used to search the Internet were...
✓ I have discovered that...
✓ My conclusions are that...
✓ I have kept my research relevant by...
✓ I found ICT helpful when...

From Design Specification to Product Specification

A design specification is a series of statements that describe the possibilities and restrictions of the product. A product specification includes details about the features and appearance of the final design, together with its materials, components and manufacturing processes.

Writing a Design Specification

The **design specification** is a very important document. It describes the things about the design which are fixed and also defines the things which you are free to change.

The conclusions from your research should form the starting point for you specification. For example, if in your conclusions you wrote:

'From the measurements I made of a number of people's backs I discovered that the best size for the length of my design would be between 30 and 50 cm.'

In the specification you would simply write:

'The garments should be between 30 and 50 cm long.'

The contents of the specification will vary according to the particular product you are designing, but on the opposite page is a checklist of aspects to consider. Don't be surprised if the specification is quite lengthy. It could easily contain 20 or more statements.

Fixing it
Some statements in the specification will be very specific, e.g.: *'It must be red.'*

Other statements may be very open ended, e.g.: *'The fabric can be of any sort.'*

Most will come somewhere in between, e.g.: *'The garnment must appeal to teenagers, and be easy to clean.'*

In this way the statements make it clear what is already fixed (e.g. the colour), and what development is required through experimentation, testing, and modification (e.g. the type of fabric and its shape, size and finish).

Writing a Product Specification

After you have fully developed your product you will need to write a final more detailed **product specification**. This time the precise statements about the materials, components and manufacturing processes will help ensure that the manufacturer is able to make a repeatable, consistent product.

Your final product will need to be evaluated against your design specification to see how closely you have been able to meet its requirements, and against your product specification to see if you have made it correctly.

don't forget...

You might find it helpful to start to rough out the design specification first, and then tackle the conclusions to your research. Working backwards, a sentence in your conclusion might need to read:

'From my survey, I discovered that young children are particularly attracted by the colour red.'

It's a good idea to use a word processor to write the specification. After you've written the design specification new information may come to light. If it will improve the final product, you can always change any of the statements.

Make sure you include as much numerical data as possible in your design specification. Try to provide data for anything which can be measured, such as size, weight, quantity, time and temperature.

Specification Checklist

The following checklist is for general guidance. Not all topics will apply to your project. You may need to explore some of these topics further during your product development.

Use and performance
Write down the main purpose of the product – what it is intended to do. Also define any other particular requirements, such as speed of operation, special features, accessories, etc. Ergonomic information is important here.

Size and weight
The minimum and maximum size and weight will be influenced by things such as the components needed and the situation the product will be used and kept in.

Generally the smaller and lighter something is the less material it will use, reducing the production costs. Smaller items can be more difficult to make, however, increasing the production costs.

Appearance
What shapes, colours and textures will be most suitable for the type of person who is likely to use the product? Remember that different people like different things.

These decisions will have an important influence on the materials and manufacturing processes, and are also crucial to ensure final sales.

Safety
A product needs to conform to all the relevant safety standards.
● Which of them will apply to your design?
● How might the product be mis-used in a potentially dangerous way?
● What warning instructions and labels need to be provided?

Conforming to the regulations can increase production costs significantly, but is an area that cannot be compromised.

Manufacturing cost
This is concerned with establishing the maximum total manufacturing cost which will allow the product to be sold at a price the consumer or client is likely to pay.

The specification needs to include details of:
● the total number of units likely to be made
● the rate of production and, if appropriate
● the size of batches.

Maintenance
Products which are virtually maintenance free are more expensive to produce.
● How frequently will different parts of the product need to be cleaned/laundered?
● How easy does this need to be?

Life expectancy
The durability of the product has a great influence on the quantity of materials and components and manufacturing process which will need to be used.

How long should the product remain in working order, providing it is used with reasonable care?

Environmental requirements
In your specification you will need to take into account how your product can be made in the most environmentally friendly way. You might decide to:
● specify maximum amounts of some materials
● avoid a particular material because it can't be easily recycled
● state the use of a specific manufacturing process because it consumes less energy.

Other areas
Other statements you might need to make might cover special requirements such as transportation and packaging.

in my design folder

✓ My design will need to...
✓ The requirements of the people who will use it are...
✓ It will also need to do the following...
✓ It will be no larger than...
✓ It will be no smaller than...
✓ Its maximum weight can be...
✓ It should not be lighter than...
✓ The shapes, colours and textures should...
✓ The design will need to conform to the following safety requirements...
✓ The number to be printed or made is...
✓ The following parts of the product should be easily replaceable...
✓ To reduce wastage and pollution it will be necessary to ensure that...

Generating and Developing Ideas

When you start designing you need lots of ideas – as many as possible, however crazy they might seem. Then you need to start to narrow things down a bit by working in more detail and evaluating what you are doing.

Work towards making at least one prototype to test some specific features of your design out. Record the results and continue to refine your ideas as much as you can. Sorting out the final details often requires lots of ideas too.

First Thoughts

Start by exploring possibilities at a very general level. Spend time doing some of the following:

▷ Brainstorming, using key words and phrases or questions which relate to the problem.

▷ Completing spider-diagrams which map out a series of ideas.

▷ Using random word or object-association to spark off new directions.

▷ Thinking up some good analogies to the situation (i.e. What is it like?).

▷ Work from an existing solution by changing some of the elements.

▷ Experimenting with some materials.

Continue doing this until you have at least two or three possible approaches to consider. Make sure they are all completely different, and not just a variation on one idea.

Go back to your design specification. Which of your approaches are closest to the statements you made? Make a decision about which idea to take further, and write down the reasons for your choice.

As you work through this section it is important to remember the following sequence when considering potential solutions:

● record a number of different possibilities
● consider and evaluate each idea
● select one approach as the best course of action, stating why.

There are lots of different drawing techniques which you can use to help you explore and develop your ideas, such as plans, elevations, sections, axonometrics, perspectives, etc.
Try to use as rich a mixture of them as possible. At this stage they should really be 'rough', rather than 'formal' (i.e. drawn with a ruler). Colour is most useful for highlighting interesting ideas.

don't forget...

As usual, it is essential to record all your ideas and thoughts.

Much of your work, particularly early on, will be in the form of notes. These need to be neat enough for the examiner to be able to read.

*Drawings on their own do not reveal very well what you had in mind, or whether you thought it was a good idea or not.
Words on their own suggest that you are not thinking visually enough.
Aim to use both sketches and words.*

As you develop your ideas, make sure you are considering the following:

- Design – aesthetics, ergonomics, marketing potential, etc.
- User requirements – functions and features.
- Technical viability – if it could be made.
- Manufacturing potential – how it could be made in quantity.
- Environmental concerns – if it can be reused, recycled, etc.?

Second Thoughts

Working on paper, begin to develop your ideas in more detail. Remember to use a range of drawing techniques, such as plans, elevations, 3D sketches, as well as words and numbers to help you model your ideas. Wherever possible, consider using a CAD program. Don't forget to print out the various stages you work through, or at least make sure you keep your own copy on disk of the screens you generate.

Planning and Making Prototypes

At some stage you will be in a position to bring your ideas into sharper focus by making some form of mock-up or prototype. Think carefully about exactly what aspect of your idea you want to test out and about the sort of model which will be most appropriate.

Whatever the form of your final outcome, the prototype might need to be:

▷ two-dimensional
▷ three-dimensional
▷ at a different scale
▷ made using different materials.

Try to devise some objective tests to carry out on your prototype involving measuring something. Don't rely just on people's opinions. Write up the circumstances in which the tests were undertaken, and record your results.

Write down some clear statements about:

▷ what you wanted the prototype to test
▷ the experimental conditions
▷ what you discovered
▷ what decisions you took about your design as a result.

Following your first prototype you may decide to modify it in some way and test it again, or maybe make a second, improved version from scratch. Make sure you keep all the prototypes you make, and ideally take photographs of them being tested perhaps using a digital camera.

Sometimes you will need to go back to review the decisions you made earlier, and on other occasions you may need to jump ahead for a while to explore new directions or to focus down on a particular detail. Make sure you have worked at both a general and a detailed level.

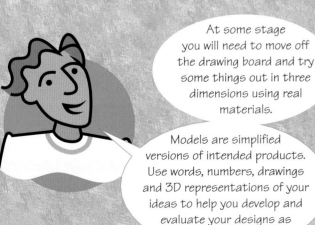

At some stage you will need to move off the drawing board and try some things out in three dimensions using real materials.

Models are simplified versions of intended products. Use words, numbers, drawings and 3D representations of your ideas to help you develop and evaluate your designs as they progress.

in my design folder

✓ I chose this idea because...
✓ I developed this aspect of my design by considering...
✓ To evaluate my ideas I decided to make a prototype which...
✓ The way I tested my prototype was to...
✓ What I discovered was...
✓ As a result I decided to change...
✓ I used ICT to...

Planning the Making and the Manufacturing

The final realisation is very important. It presents your proposed design solution rather than the process you used to develop it. Careful planning is essential. You will also need to be able to explain how your product could be reproduced or manufactured in quantity.

How many?

What you have designed should be suitable for manufacture or reproduction. You should discuss with your teacher how many items you should attempt to make. This is likely to depend on the complexity of your design and the materials and facilities available in your workshops. It may be that you only make one item, but also provide a clear account of how a quantity of them could be produced.

keeping a record

Write up a diary record of the progress you made while making. Try to include references to:

● things you did to ensure safety
● the appropriate use of materials
● minimising wastage
● choosing tools
● practising making first
● checking that what you are making is accurate enough to work
● asking experts (including teachers) for advice explaining why you had to change your original plan for making.

A Plan of Action

Before you start planning you will need to ensure that you have a final artwork rough of your design. You will also need a diagram of a pattern for your design (see pages 48–49). This must include all pattern markings, measurements and materials to be used. Ideally there should also be written and drawn instructions which would enable someone else to be able to make up the design from your plans.

Next work out a production flow chart as follows.

1 List the order in which you will prepare the final artwork or make the main parts of the product. Include as much detail as you can (see page 124).

2 Divide the list up into a number of main stages, e.g. gathering materials and components, preparing (i.e. marking out, cutting), assembling, finishing.

3 Identify series of operations which might be done in parallel.

4 Indicate the time scale involved on an hourly, daily and weekly basis.

Think carefully about what equipment is available in your school.

don't forget...

You may find you have to change your plans as you go. There is nothing wrong with doing this, but you should explain why you have had to adjust your schedule, and show that you have considered the likely effect of the later stages of production.

Try using the planning techniques described on page 125.

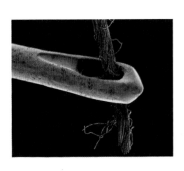

Quality Counts

As your making proceeds you will need to check frequently that your work is of acceptable quality. How accurately will you need to work? What tolerances will be acceptable? (See page 130.) How can you judge the quality of the finish? What might cause a product to be rejected?

If you are making a number of identical items you should try and work out ways of checking the quality through a sampling process (see page 130).

Making

While you are in the process of making you must ensure that the tools and materials you are using are the correct ones. Pay particular attention to safety instructions and guidelines.

Try to ensure that you have a finished item at the end, even if it involves simplifying what you do.

Aim to produce something which is made and finished as accurately as possible. If necessary you may need to develop and practise certain skills beforehand.

Planning for Manufacture

Manufacturing matters

Try asking the following questions about the way your design might be made in quantity:

- What work operation is being carried out, and why? What alternatives might there be?
- Where is the operation done, and why? Where else might it be carried out?
- When is it done, and why? When else might it be undertaken?
- Who carries it out, and why? Who else might do it?
- How is it undertaken, and why, How else might it be done?

Remember that manufacturing is not just about making things. It is also about making them better by making them:
- simpler • quicker
- cheaper • more efficient
- less damaging to the environment.

Try to explain how your product would be manufactured in quantity. Work through the following stages:

1 Determine which type of production will be most suitable, depending on the number to be made.
2 Break up the production process into its major parts and identify the various sub-assemblies.
3 Consider where jigs, templates and moulding processes could be used. Where could 2D or 3D CAM be effectively used?
4 Make a list of the total number of components and volume of raw material needed for the production run.

5 Identify which parts will be made by the company and which will need to be bought in ready-made from outside suppliers.
6 Draw up a production schedule which details the manufacturing process to ensure that the materials and components will be available exactly where and when needed. How should the workforce and workspace be arranged?
7 Decide how quality control systems will be applied to

produce the degree of accuracy required.
8 Determine health and safety issues and plan to minimise risks.
9 Calculate the manufacturing cost of the product.
10 Review the design of the product and manufacturing process to see if costs can be reduced.

More information on all these topics can be found on pages 122 to 133.

> Remember to use a wide range of graphic techniques to help plan and explain your making.

> Don't forget that there is also a high proportion of marks for demonstrating skill and accuracy, overcoming difficulties and working safely during the making.

> What needs to be done by:
> - next month
> - next week
> - next lesson
> - the end of this lesson?

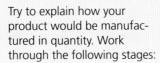

in my design folder

✓ I planned the following sequence of making...
✓ I had to change my plan to account for...
✓ I used the following equipment and processes...
✓ I paid particular attention to safety by...
✓ I monitored the quality of my product by...
✓ I used CAD-CAM to...

Testing and Evaluation

You will need to find out how successful your final design solution is. How well does it match the design specification? How well have you worked? What would you do differently if you had another chance?

As you work through your project you will regularly carry out testing and evaluation. For example:

▷ analysing and evaluating the research material you collected.

▷ evaluating and testing carried out on existing products.

▷ evaluating initial sketche ideas or samples and models in order to make the right decisions about which to develop further.

▷ assessing the quality of your making as you go along.

Last of all you must test and evaluate your final solution.

What methods could you use to test the success of these textile products?

Testing the Final Solution

To find out how successful your design is you will need to test it out. Some of the ways in which you might do this are by:

▷ trying it out yourself

▷ asking other people to use it

▷ asking experts what they think about it.

As well as recording people's thoughts, observations and opinions, try to obtain some data: how many times it worked, over what periods of time, within what performance limits, etc?

To help you decide what to test, you should look back to the statements in your design specification, and focus on the most important ones. If for example the specification stated that a three-year-old child must be able to wear it, try and find out how many can. If it must be a colour which would appeal to young children, devise a way of finding out what age ranges it does appeal to.

You need to provide evidence to show that you have tested your final design out in some way. Try to ensure that your findings relate directly to the statements in your original specification. Include as much information and detail as you can.

don't forget...

Don't be too surprised or worried if your design isn't perfect – the important thing is that you can identify what needs improving. Can you make some simple suggestions about how it might be improved?

Final Evaluation

There are two things you need to discuss in the final evaluation: the quality of the product you have designed, and the process you went through while designing it.

The product

How successful is your final design? Comment on:

▷ how it compares with your original intentions as stated in your design specification
▷ how well it solves the original problem
▷ the materials you used
▷ what it looks like
▷ how well it works
▷ what a potential user said
▷ what experts said
▷ whether it could be reproduced or manufactured cheaply enough in quantity to make a profit
▷ the effective use of ICT to assist reproduction or manufacture
▷ the extent to which it meets the requirements of the client, manufacturer and the retailer.
▷ the ways in which it could be improved.

Justify your evaluation by including references to what happened when you tested it.

The process

How well have you worked? Imagine you suddenly had more time, or were able to start again, and consider:

▷ Which aspects of your investigation, design development work and making would you try to improve, or approach in a different way?
▷ What did you leave to the last minute, or spend too much time on?
▷ Which parts are you most pleased with, and why?
▷ How well did you make the final realisation?
▷ How effective was your use of ICT? How did it enhance your work?

If you had more time:

● what aspects of the product would you try to improve? (refer to your evaluation if you can).
● how would you improve the way you had researched, developed, planned and evaluated your working process?

in my design folder

What do you think you have learnt through doing the project?

✓ Comparison of my final product specification with my design specification showed that...
✓ The people I showed my ideas (drawings and final product) to said...
✓ I was able to try my design out by...
✓ I discovered that...
✓ I could improve it by...
✓ I didn't do enough research into...
✓ I spent too long on...
✓ I should have spent more time on...
✓ The best aspect is...
✓ I have learnt a lot about...
✓ ICT helped me to...

Try to identify a mixture of good and bad points about your final proposal and method of working. You will gain credit for being able to demonstrate that you are aware of weaknesses in what you have designed and the way that you have designed it.

If people have been critical of aspects of your design, do you agree with them? Explain your response.

Don't forget to write about both the product and the process.

Remember that evaluation is on-going. It should also appear throughout your project whenever decisions are made. Explain the reasons behind your actions.

Project Presentation

The way you present your project work is extremely important. Remember you won't be there to explain it all when it's being assessed! You need to make it as easy as possible for an examiner to see and understand what you have done.

Telling the Story

All your investigation and development work needs to be handed in at the end, as well as what you have made. Your design folder needs to tell the story of the project. Each section should lead on from the next, and clearly show what happened next, and explain why. Section titles and individual page titles can help considerably. Try to ensure you have at least one A3 sheet which covers each of the headings shown opposite.

There is no single way in which you must present your work, but the following suggestions are all highly recommended:

▷ Securely bind all the pages together in some way. Use staples or treasury tags. There is no need to buy an expensive folder.
▷ Add a cover with a title and an appropriate illustration.
▷ Make it clear which the main sections are.
▷ Add in titles or running headings to each sheet to indicate what aspect of the design you were considering at that particular point in the project.

Remember to include evidence of ICT work and other Key Skills. Carefully check through your folder and correct any spelling and punctuation mistakes.

Presenting your Design Project Sheets

▷ Always work on standard-size paper, either A3 or A4.

▷ Aim to have a good mixture of text and visual images. These could be produced by hand, or on a computer.

▷ You might like to design a special border to use on each sheet.

▷ Include as many different types of illustration as possible.

▷ When using photographs, use a small amount of adhesive applied evenly all the way round the edge to secure them to your design folder sheet. A small amount of paper adhesive applied evenly all the way round the edge is the best way of fixing them on.

▷ Think carefully about the lettering for titles, and don't just put them anywhere and anyhow. Try to choose a height and width of lettering which will be well balanced on the whole page. If the title is too big or boldly coloured it may dominate the sheet. If it is thin or light it might not be noticed.

don't forget...

Presentation is something you need to be thinking about throughout your project work.

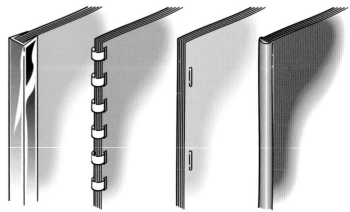

Binding methods

Presenting your Project Report

You may decide to also hand in a final **project report**. This would be a more formal document and used to, for example:

▷ describe and discuss the development process
▷ document detailed research material
▷ evaluate your project in detail.

If possible, type up the report, using a word processor, or a DTP program. Remember to think carefully about the design of the layout of text, and to include illustrations such as statistical graphs and charts, technical drawings and photographs, as appropriate.

Your project report could include:

● a cover
● an introduction
● your investigation and development
● test results
● your final evaluation
● an appendix.

Project One: Introduction

A local theatre director intends to stage a production of Gilbert and Sullivan's The Mikado *next season. He is looking for someone to design and make some costumes and some fabrics for the stage set.*

Designing for the Theatre (page 32)

Putting it Together (page 52)

Cutting it out (page 50)

Read the following letter carefully:

With reference to our recent meeting I am pleased to confirm that we would like to commission you to produce the costumes and fabrics for our forthcoming production of *The Mikado*.

We intend to have a very simple stage set, and to use the shapes, colours and patterns of the costumes, screens, banners and other fabric items to bring the opera alive.

We will need to receive from you:
- initial ideas for the costumes
- test pieces
- a sample costume for one of the main characters and/or
- a sample fabric for the stage set.

Enclosed is a brief outline of the story and descriptions of the main characters and one of the scenes which will be required.

I look forward to seeing your ideas and discussing their potential at our first production meeting.

Yours sincerely

Theatre Director

Clarifying the Brief

▷ Make a list of all the things the theatre director expects you to do.

▷ Read the **story outline** and descriptions of the **characters** and **scenes**, which you will find on page 30–1.

Creating an effect with Colour (page 36)

Embellishing Fabrics (page 40)

ON STAGE

Colouring Fabric (page 42)

Adapting a Pattern (page 48)

Visual Research

You will need to start looking out for examples of Japanese costumes and sketch examples of **accessories**, **surface patterns** and **motifs**.

Use the Internet to help.

First Thoughts

Brainstorm your initial thoughts and ideas using labelled sketches and/or spider diagrams.

▷ What might the costumes be like?
▷ How could textiles be used effectively as part of the stage set?

ON STAGE

starting point

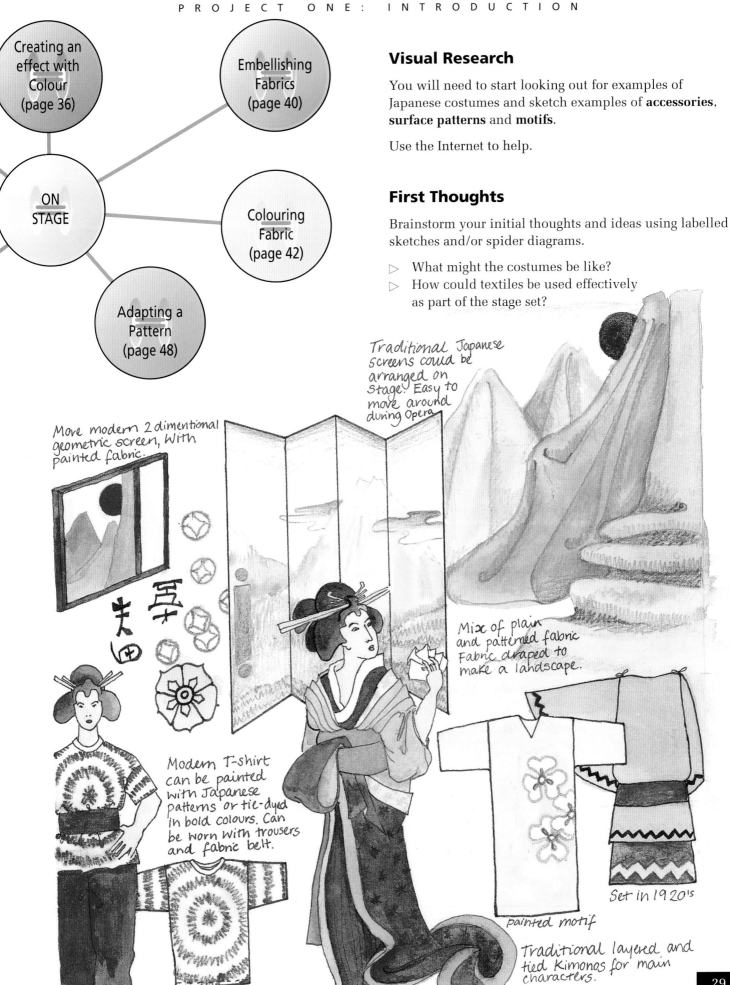

More modern 2 dimensional geometric screen, With painted fabric.

Traditional Japanese screens could be arranged on stage. Easy to move around during Opera.

Mix of plain and patterned fabric. Fabric draped to make a landscape.

Modern T-shirt can be painted with Japanese patterns or tie-dyed in bold colours. Can be worn with trousers and fabric belt.

Set in 1920's

painted motif

Traditional layered and tied Kimonos for main characters.

29

The Mikado

Understanding the atmosphere, setting and main characters of the storyline is vital to the successful design of costumes and stage-sets.

You will need to make notes on the following:

▷ Where is the musical set?
▷ What **period** is it set in?
▷ What is the **mood** of the story?
▷ What are the **personalities** of the main characters?

If you prefer you could choose to design your costumes for a different play or musical. You will need to obtain similar information about the **characters** and **settings**.

About *The Mikado*

The Mikado has always been the most popular of all Gilbert and Sullivan's works. It was first performed on the 14th March 1885 in London. During the 1880s, when it was written, Britain was swept by a craze for everything Japanese, and the comic opera provided the opportunity for some splendid costumes and exotic scenery.

Although set in a mythical Japanese village, *The Mikado* is in fact a satire on 19th century Britain. For example, *The Mikado*'s ideas of appropriate punishments include forcing railway vandals to travel on exceedingly slow trains!

Revival of the Mikado at the Savoy Theatre, 1896

Enter procession of YUM-YUM's school fellows, heralding YUM-YUM, PEEP-BO, and PITTI-SING

THE THREE   Three little maids from school are we,
Pert as a schoolgirl well can be,
Filled to the brim with girlish glee,
Three little maids from school.

YUM-YUM   Everything is a source of fun
PEEP-BO   Nobody's safe, for we care for none!
PITTI-SING   Life is a joke that's just begun
THE THREE   Three little maids from school!
All (dancing)   Three little maids who, all awary,
Come from a ladies' seminary,
Freed from its genius tutelary –

THE THREE (suddenly demure). Three little maids from school!

The Characters and the Plot

The storyline and characters are wildly improbable.

▷ The Mikado is the very grand Emperor of Japan.
▷ Nanki-Poo is the Mikado's son. He disguises himself as a wandering minstrel in order to escape the attentions of Katisha.
▷ Katisha, a brazen, grotesque and blood-thirsty elderly lady, is determined to marry Nanki-Poo.
▷ Yum-Yum is the schoolgirl who Nanki-Poo falls in love with, but she is already engaged to Ko-Ko.
▷ Ko-Ko is the flirtatious Lord High Executioner.

The other main characters include Pooh-Bah (the Lord High Everything Else) and Pish-Tush (an officious nobleman), and a chorus of School Girls, Nobles, Guards and Coolies.

After a series of misunderstandings Nanki-Poo eventually gets to marry Yum-Yum, and Ko-Ko avoids marrying Katisha.

The scenes

Act 1 is set in the courtyard of Ko-Ko's palace in Titipu. Act II is in Ko-Ko's garden

The setting – Japanese style

In the second half of the 19th Century the Japanese were adapting to Western practices, altering their social and legal rules, their clothing, and the whole outlook of their country.

Hairstyles were the easiest and cheapest to alter. In 1873 the Emperor set a trend by having his 'top-knot' cut off. It was increasingly common at this time to see Japanese people dressed in a combination of Western dress and a traditional kimono.

For centuries Japanese women had sewn their own and their family's clothes. In contrast to the simple design of the kimono, Western dress was complicated and required a totally different way of sewing. At first only the very rich could afford to alter their style of dress.

■ ACTIVITY

Find out more about the ways in which Western and Japanese cultures were influenced by each other during the second half of the 19th Century. What part did the new printing, production and transport technologies of the time play?

Designing for the Theatre (1)

ON STAGE

Designing theatrical costumes is not the same as designing garments for everyday life. Different fabrics and methods of production are needed.

19th Century Victorian dress

Costume Design

One of the most important features of **costume design** is that the garments look distinctive from a distance. They may have to contrast or harmonise with other costumes, or with the scenery. To achieve this you may need to use fabrics, colours and decorations that would not normally be used for everyday wear.

Costumes may need to reflect a particular culture or period of history. At the same time they might be for a character who lives in great wealth or extreme poverty, in which case the garments could be very elaborate, or threadbare.

Sometimes costumes need to help emphasise the nature of the character being played. For example, visual references to a lion could help represent someone who can become angry and ferocious, yet is also majestic.

Victorian woman

Georgian dress 1700–1790

Production Methods

For the main characters only one copy of a costume design will be required. This type of **production** is described as '**one-off**'. It might be made by one person, or a small group of people.

Some productions have large crowd scenes, or a chorus where the costumes required are the same or very similar. In this case a '**batch**' system of production would be used. This would involve several people working together, sharing the tasks and the equipment to make a number of very similar garments. Patterns would be carefully worked out to ensure minimum wastage and some parts would be cut together to save time.

Costumes have to be easy to put on (particularly if a 'quick change' is needed between scenes) and easy to maintain as they are likely to get dirty or torn quite quickly. It is also essential that they are comfortable to wear and easy to move around in.

Setting the Scene

Settings can be made from many materials. Metals, plastics, wood and fabrics are all used to create **stage sets**. Things are not always what they seem, however. Many surfaces are painted on to a flat wood or canvas, and textures and shadows added to give the effect of different materials.

Sometimes there is very little actual 'scenery'. The clever use of props, costumes and lighting on their own can be enough to create the mood and atmosphere of the setting.

Single sets are the easiest to design. Changes of scenery present a more demanding challenge.

The role of the set designer is to:

▷ represent the play's atmosphere
▷ allow enough space for the actors to move or dance
▷ to ensure that the performers are always visible
▷ create scenery which can be changed quickly and easily
▷ work within the budget.

The effectiveness and originality of the solutions to these problems are a measure of the success and skill of the designer.

Designing with Fabrics

Flowing fabric

Explore the use of fabrics as loose banners, streamers, hand-held flags or long ribbons (like those used by gymnasts). You might create fans of different shapes out of the fabric, and paint motifs on them to represent the place of the action or to reinforce the character.

Think about long strips of fabric hung from the ceiling, or 'flown-in', i.e. tied to long battens or poles which can be raised or lowered on ropes. These strips can be painted with scenes or motifs. They could be front or back lit. If lit from the front they can create areas of strong colour or help provide a focal point for a scene. When lit from the back some materials will become transparent, allowing the audience to see silhouettes.

Free-standing fabric

Experiment with the possibilities of using **free-standing flats**. These are made from fabric stretched over a wooden frame. They are then stiffened with glue and resin to form a hard surface for painting. The most common size for a base flat is 4 metres high by 2 metres wide. You could create scale models of scenes in one quarter size.

Alternatively, other free-standing shapes such as squares, pyramids and triangles can be covered with a variety of fabrics to give them a surface texture or design. The advantage of this is that the shapes can be used again easily .

Fabric fields

Fabric can be used effectively to represent the sea, a river, a field or a garden by placing it loosely on the floor. The actors could, for example, then use it to play out a scene where there is a shipwreck, gradually lifting it so that it covers their heads so that it appears as if they are drowning.

I had been commissioned to design the sets and costumes for the 'Diary of a Noblewoman', a play which only has one character, a Japanese noblewoman who appears at six different stages of her life.

I used muslin for the costume and muslin drapes for the set. The character added a new piece of material to her kimono for each new scene. Each layer was a shade of jade blue which got deeper as the character aged, but left a lower border of the lighter colour.

The muslin drapes gave colour washes of blues and magenta. These were sometimes backlit to show a formal Japanese garden in silhouette.

KEY POINTS

● There are some important differences between designing theatrical costumes and garments to be worn for everyday life.
● One-off or batch production is used to make costumes for the theatre.

Designing for the Theatre (2)

ON STAGE

You will find it helpful to study some existing costumes and compare them with ordinary clothes.

Dressing Mr Jolly

'I work as a designer for television programmes and commercials. Recently I was asked to create the costumes for the characters and puppets for a children's programme.

The main character was called 'Mr Jolly'. During the programme he acts the part of other characters from nursery rhymes and stories. For one episode he needed a costume for 'The Old Woman Who Lived in a Shoe'.

The programme director felt it was important that the children still recognised Mr Jolly, even when he was dressed like a woman!

In my design I needed to take the following into consideration:

▶ the character
▶ what action the script required the character to do
▶ what fabrics, colours and styles would work well with Mr Jolly's original costume.

▶ the general visual style of the programme
▶ how quickly the costume had to be put on and taken off
▶ the age of the viewers
▶ the available budget
▶ when it needed to be ready by.

The idea I came up with was to use Mr Jolly's original yellow shirt and purple trousers and add a pinafore, cap, wig and glasses.

The costume needed to look 'larger than life' and like a pantomime dame. I used exaggerated colours and patterns and included an outsize pocket for Mr Jolly to hide his props in, as required by the script. Simple accessories were used to keep the time for changing to a minimum, and to keep the whole costume easy and cheap to make.'

Product Analysis

You will need to make a comparison between the way in which **stage costumes** and **everyday garments** are designed, constructed and finished. Examining existing products in detail and taking them apart to discover how they have been assembled is a good way to do this.

See if you can obtain a stage costume – if not base your study on the one shown on the right. You will also need a discarded garment such as a pair of trousers, a jacket or a shirt. Ideally it should have some form of decoration or interesting fastenings on it.

Make sketches of the back, front and inside of the garments. You may find it helpful to turn them inside out.

Examine the garments carefully and draw a diagram of all the pattern pieces which would have been needed to make them.

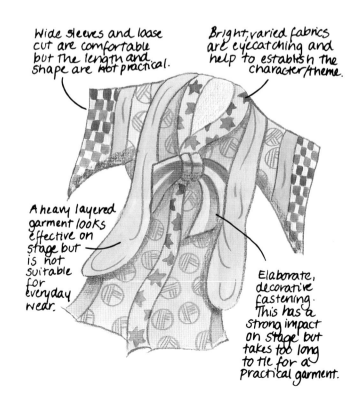

Wide sleeves and loose cut are comfortable but the length and shape are not practical.

Bright, varied fabrics are eyecatching and help to establish the character/theme.

A heavy layered garment looks effective on stage but is not suitable for everyday wear.

Elaborate, decorative fastening. This has a strong impact on stage but takes too long to tie for a practical garment.

How would you describe the everyday garment?

▷ What sort of person might wear it and on what sort of occasions?
▷ What moods and feeling do any colours, textures or patterns suggest?
▷ Where are the seams?
▷ What fabrics have been used, and how might they have been printed or dyed?

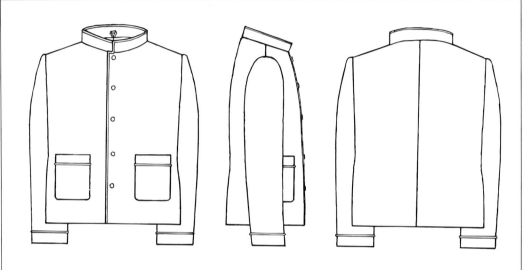

▷ Are there any materials which cannot be seen from the outside?
▷ What trimmings and fastenings have been used?
▷ Where are the brand and manufacturer's labels and what information do they provide?
▷ Is the garment in good condition?

Do you think it is a successful piece of design?

▷ What are the good points and bad points about the design?
▷ Can you suggest any improvements?
▷ How well has it survived wear and tear, and being cleaned?
▷ Is it still 'in fashion'?

Apply the questions above to the stage costume.

▷ Which ones are not relevant?
▷ Which produce contrasting answers to those for the everyday garment?

Write a conclusion which summarises the similarities and differences in the designs of stage costumes and everyday garments.

You could use a paint or graphics CAD program to develop a range of designs. These can be printed either directly onto paper and or fabric.

IN YOUR PROJECT

▶ Describe and evaluate a traditional Japanese costume. Sketch textile prints, patterns, colours and the shape of garments. Make small sketches of the pattern pieces they might have used. Sketch and colour some typical Japanese textile prints.
▶ See if you can think of anyone who might have seen a performance of *The Mikado*. It would be interesting to hear what they thought about its costumes and staging.
▶ Are there any videos of *The Mikado* you can watch?

ON STAGE

design disassembly

Shoulder seam. The cut is smart, comfortable and practical.

Hanging loop. Practical for storage.

Armhole.

Button holes.

Facing.

Lining.

Care label Easy care fabric.

Piping in contrasting colour. Smart details emphasise the simple cut.

Patch pocket with top stitching. Strong and practical.

Buttons. Easy to use, a strong and practical fastening.

Creating an Effect with Colour

ON STAGE

Colour can be used to create all sorts of dramatic effects. It can alter the way we feel by creating different moods. Colours can be in harmony or contrast with each other.

Japanese Noh theatre costume

Colour Associations

Traditionally the colour of clothing has been considered highly significant. It is often used to create distinction between the sexes and classes. For example, the ancient Persians restricted the number of colours women were allowed to wear. Today we still associate blue with a baby boy and pink with a baby girl.

In Western cultures these distinctions have largely disappeared, but in some societies, such as India for example, colour is still invested with symbolic meaning.

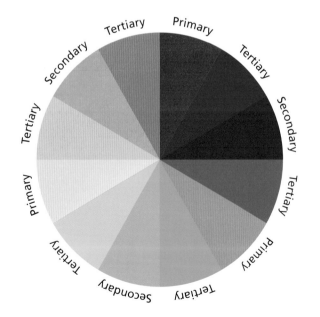

100%   0%

The Colour Wheel

▷ The **primary colours** are red, blue and yellow.
▷ The **secondary colours** are purple, green and orange. These are produced by mixing two primary colours together.
▷ The **tertiary colours** are produced by mixing a primary colour with an adjacent secondary colour.
▷ **Complementary colours** are opposite each other on the colour wheel (e.g. blue and orange). These colours create contrast.
▷ **Harmonious colours** are close to each other on the colour wheel. These colours create harmony.
▷ A single colour (e.g. red) is described as the **hue**.
▷ The hue can be changed by adding white to make it lighter (a **tone**), or black to make it darker (a **shade**).
▷ The reds, yellows and oranges on one side of the colour circle are known as '**warm' colours**, while the blues and greens opposite are called '**cold' colours**.

Eastern Influences

During the nineteenth century a number of international exhibitions were held in Europe. The designs of the Japanese had an enormous impact on Western approaches to colour, composition and design. Many artists collected Japanese woodcuts and artefacts and based their own designs on patterns and unusual colour combinations such as turquoise and coral.

The decorations of Japanese Noh costumes influenced artists such as Gustav Klimt. He had his own collection, and their influence can be seen in his paintings. His figures are often dressed in colourful and decorative robes.

Fulfilment by Gustav Klimt (1862–1918)

■ ACTIVITY

Look closely at the Noh costume and the work of Gustav Klimt. Use them as the basis for a series of sample patterns using either:

▶ harmonious colours, or
▶ contrasting colours.

IN YOUR PROJECT

Suggest and describe the type of colours needed for the production. Suggest some special effects which could be created by the lighting.

KEY POINTS

- Traditionally colour has always been invested with significance.
- Colours are either primary, secondary or tertiary.
- Colours can be used to create harmony and contrast.
- Colour is always affected by light and texture.
- Fabric texture can influence its effect on stage.

ON STAGE

enhancement of fabrics

On Stage

Colour

By using different colours and types of light on stage it is possible to vary the colours of the costumes and scenery without actually changing them.

Different types of light alter the colours of the things they illuminate: at different times of the day and year, sunlight can range from a golden brown to harsh yellow or bright blue. There are also different types of artificial light. For example, the colour red will appear to be:

▷ orange under a tungsten light
▷ bluish under a fluorescent tube
▷ brown under a yellow sodium street lamp
▷ black under a green mercury lamp.

At the same time the hue of the actor's skin will alter under different kinds of lighting.

The colours of costumes also need to be considered in relation to the colours of the set.

These are very important considerations when designing for the theatre.

Texture

Fabrics have **texture** as well as colour. Decorative techniques such as collages and three-dimensional effects may 'catch the light' and create a shimmering effect. Gold and other metallic fabrics and threads may enhance this effect. Some fabrics, such as satin weaves, 'shine' more than others because their smooth surface reflects the light.

Techniques for creating unusual textures are presented on pages 40 to 44.

Writing a Design Specification/Developing Ideas

A design brief is the general statement of what the company or client requires. A specification is compiled by the designer after the client's needs have been clarified. It is a list of possibilities and restrictions and it allows the designer to think of the final outcome in more detail.

It was good to meet up with you yesterday and to see your first ideas.

I hope it is now clearer as to exactly what we require, and that you can now go on to develop your ideas in more detail. Just remember that I'm depending on you to come up with something stunning! I'm greatly looking forward to seeing your final proposals at our next meeting.

Until then

Writing a Design Specification

Begin by looking through all your research and write a short conclusion. This should help you focus on things about your design which are fixed and those you will be able to change. For example there may be strict limitations on using a particular technique if it is too costly or too time-consuming. Consider the areas below.

Function
Which character is your costume going to be for, or which scene is your fabric for? What particular requirements are there?

Aesthetics
You need to think about the overall visual appearance of your design. This is what people will notice first and what they think and feel is important. It includes things such as line, colour, texture, finish, style, shape, form, size, proportion, decoration and patterns. This is not fixed. It will be possible to experiment with many different ideas.

Safety
Considerations should always be given to the user of the finished item and the environment in which it will be used. There is legislation which sets safety standards for textile items which have been developed to protect the consumer. Your costume is slightly different in that it will not go on sale to the general public but safety must still be considered.

Materials
Durability: how hard-wearing does this garment have to be? How often will it be worn?
Maintenance: how often will the garment need to be washed, dried and ironed? Will it be possible to have it dry-cleaned?
Aesthetic properties: will the fabric need to drape well or have texture? At this stage the material to be used is up to you to choose.

Cost
Always an important consideration, it will have a great influence on the materials, trimmings and manufacturing processes used. Materials are usually the most expensive consideration when designing something in school. In industry, labour costs are also very high and the final design will depend a lot on what the client is willing to spend. At this stage you may be able to say, 'It must cost no more than...'

Design Specification
- My costume is for Katisha
- The colours must be...
- The style and shape must be...
- The material must be...
- Safety aspects include...
- It must cost no more than...
- It must co-ordinate with the rest of the production.

■ ACTIVITY

In your project folder write a specification for your design. State what is fixed and what you are free to experiment with.

Developing Initial Design Ideas

embroidered back panel.
YUM YUM
quilted waistband
Fabric samples
tie dye circles
zip decorating
applique circle
section of embroidery

Textile techniques

Now you have completed a thorough investigation you will need to become more familiar with a range of textile techniques, such as:

▷ embellishment (see pages 40 to 43) and
▷ colouring fabrics (see pages 44 to 47).

Make sure you do the activities and practise your skills. You will be able to use your knowledge to develop more sophisticated designs.

Exploring possible ideas

At this stage try not to form fixed ideas about what you will eventually make. Use notes and quick sketches to get your ideas down. Do not be too fussy about your drawings. Remember to:

▷ annotate...
▷ suggest...
▷ show...
▷ suggest...

Second thoughts

Look carefully at your ideas and evaluate them. Look again at your specification and remind yourself of any limitations to your final design, such as cost.

▷ Note down your thoughts in your project folder.
▷ Discuss your ideas with your teacher and friends.

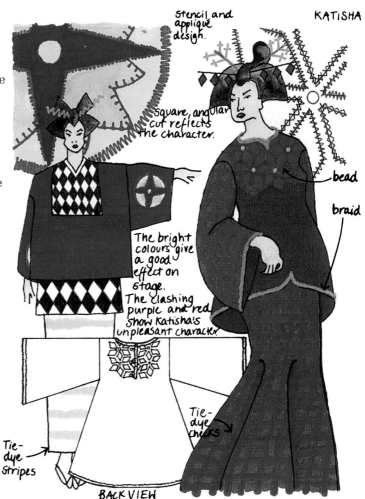

KATISHA

Stencil and appliqué design.

Square, angular cut reflects the character.

bead

braid

The bright colours give a good effect on stage. The clashing purple and red show Katisha's unpleasant character.

Tie-dye stripes

Tie-dye checks

BACK VIEW

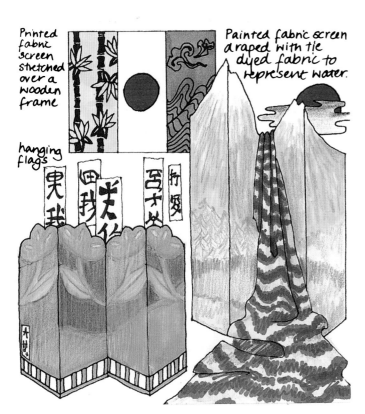

Printed fabric screen stretched over a wooden frame

hanging flags

Painted fabric screen draped with tie dyed fabric to represent water.

Developing a final idea

Develop what you consider to be your most promising idea in more detail. You will need to think about:

▷ adapting a pattern (see pages 48 to 49)
▷ cutting out (see page 50 to 51) and
▷ planning the making of the final product (see pages 54 to 55).

For the final meeting with the director you will also need to prepare a presentation drawing showing colour, detailed annotation and if possible small samples of fabrics you intend to use.

Make sure you give your reasons for choosing your final design idea.

Project presentation

Remember to think about the quality of presentation of the development of your design ideas. Use a variety of techniques such as mood-boards, photographs, sketches, colour-boards, swatches and test pieces.

Remember that ICT can be used to help you with the presentation.

Embellishing Fabrics (1)

ON STAGE

Embellishing means to decorate. A garment can be made more original and interesting by adding decoration. Practise new techniques such as appliqué by making up small test-pieces or samples. These will help make the texture of your designs more interesting.

Rising Sun Quilt by Mary Totten, New York c. 1830

Appliqué

Appliqué is a very old textile technique. It involves applying one piece of fabric to another in order to decorate it. The oldest existing piece of appliqué work dates from 980 BC. The technique was used throughout Europe in the Middle Ages. Necessity drove pioneers in America to produce patchwork and appliqué quilts. It is practised in cultures all over the world including India, Pakistan, Russia and Central and South America.

ICT ➡

You could use the internet or CD-Roms to find out more about:
- different types of appliqué, from around the world.
- designs from other times
- the work of contemporary textile designers

■ **ACTIVITY**

Make some samples.

Produce a simple appliqué motif.

Make a creative applique collage by experimenting with different fabric textures, stitches, threads and colour.

You will need the following: a sewing machine, needles, threads, fabric scissors, a fabric marker or tailor's chalk, scraps of different fabrics and a medium-weight woven fabric, such as calico, for the background.

1 Draw a motif onto the fabric and cut it out. You could use a design that you have already sketched or found.

2 Pin and tack the fabric motif onto the background material. If the fabric is very lightweight or stretches you may have to back stiffen it with Bonda-web or Inter-facing.

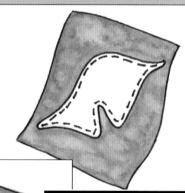

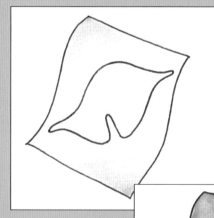

3 Set your machine on zig-zag stitch and carefully sew round your motif exactly on the raw edge of the fabric. As well as being decorative, this may also stop the edges from fraying.

Interfacing is used when making garments to strengthen things such as button stands, collars and cuffs. It may be woven, knitted or bonded and comes in many different weights so you can pick one to match your fabric.

Creating samples/test-pieces

Making samples is very useful for a number of reasons.

▷ You can find out what effects can be created by using various techniques.
▷ They enable you to experiment and have fun without worrying too much about making mistakes or things not turning out as expected.
▷ You might discover exciting ideas that you can use later on
▷ They encourage you to practise and develop your skills before making your final garment.

Textile by Susan Kennewell

Make sure you keep all your samples and include them in your design folder.

Think carefully about how to combine your experiments into a collage.

▷ Where will the different pieces be placed?
▷ Which colours and patterns will be placed together?

What overall shape will it be?

■ ACTIVITY

1. Look around your home and go through your wardrobe and look for examples of appliqué.
Illustrate them in your design folder. Describe the materials used and how effective they are.

2. Find out more about appliqué techniques by looking in the library. See if you can discover what reverse appliqué is.

3. Produce a short illustrated account of some aspect of appliqué that interests you – for example work from India or Russia.

▶ What makes it special to that country?
▶ What materials, motifs, shapes and colours are typically used?

IN YOUR PROJECT

▶ Would appliqué be a good technique to use to decorate the garment you are designing?
▶ What ideas have you got for experimenting with sample pieces?

KEY POINTS

● Use models, samples, test-pieces and CAD when developing your designs.
● Appliqué involves applying one fabric to another in order to create colourful decorative textile effects.
● Interfacing is used to strengthen fabric.
● Different stitches can be used to sew fabrics together, and can add to the decorative effect.

Embellishing Fabrics (2)

ON STAGE

There are other ways to decorate fabrics. Some can be used with appliqué either to enhance it or to create a more three-dimensional effect.

Fastenings can be decorative as well as functional.

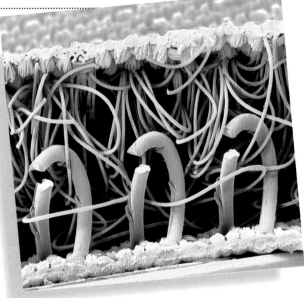

Velcro: made from woven nylon hooks and loops. (magnified x15)

Padding

Your appliqué work (or part of it) can be padded by inserting a piece of wadding or stuffing behind the fabric pieces. This creates a three-dimensional effect and can give your work added depth.

There are also more intricate and detailed effects which can be achieved by using hand and machine embroidery, sequins and beading.

Remember that very fine details may not been seen on stage unless they are made using threads and trimmings which glisten or create texture. These can be very eye-catching under stage lights.

Quilting

Quilting is a technique which can create texture and definition. It involves placing wadding between two layers of fabric and stitching on top to create a pattern.

Layering

Quilting is also one of the best ways to insulate an anorak or a bedcover. Polyester wadding is designed to trap as much air as possible within the structure of the fabric. Air is trapped between the three layers of fabric. Stitching on the three layers is kept to a minimum as too many thin areas reduces the insulation.

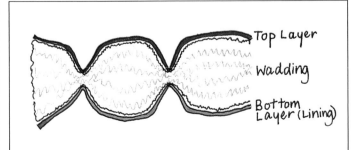

Top Layer

Wadding

Bottom Layer (Lining)

How to quilt

1 Transfer your design onto the top layer of fabric using the direct tracing method, tailor's chalk or a fabric marker pen.

2 Put the three layers of fabric together and tack them . This will prevent the fabric from puckering later on.

3 Now you can stitch around your design. By hand bring the needle through the layers of fabric from the wrong side, making sure it goes straight through and not at an angle. Push the needle straight through them again to make a small, straight stitch. Repeat this stitch to make an evenly spaced line.

It is quicker to use machine stitching. Use a fairly large straight stitch or an open zig-zag stitch.

Remove the tacking when finished.

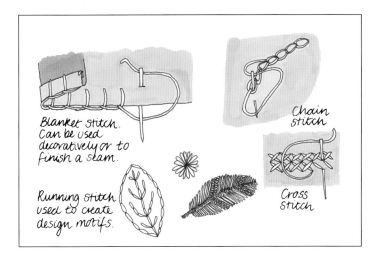

Blanket stitch. Can be used decoratively or to finish a seam.

Running stitch used to create design motifs.

Chain stitch

Cross stitch

Embroidery

To create **embroidery**, threads of different colours are stitched onto the fabric to form a pattern. This can be done by hand or by machine. Many domestic machines can produce pre-programmed patterns. The machine can also be used for free-style **machine embroidery** by dropping the feed dog, removing the presser foot and moving the fabric about under the needle while stretched in a tambour frame.

Industrial embroidery machines are often used in industry to produce badges, logos and names as well as motifs and patterns.

Fastenings

As well as being functional, **fastenings** can also be used to decorate a garment. Fastenings may need to be:

▷ wind or waterproof
▷ invisible
▷ easy to open and close
▷ strong
▷ washable.

▓ ACTIVITY

Divide the following fastenings into those which are purely functional and those which could also be decorative: Velcro, buttons, hooks and eyes, toggles, poppers, ties and bows, press studs, frogging, zips.

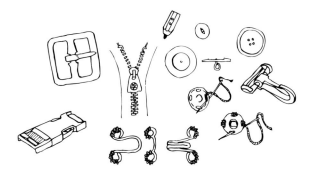

Toggles, zips and buttons used decoratively on a costume.

Pre-manufactured components

In industry manufacturers use pre-manufactured components. These include fastenings, threads, edgings, braids, pre-manufactured collars, cuffs, shoulder pads and electronic noise and movement features.

CAM (see page 128) is often used to manufacture components such as badges, motifs, logos and labels. This ensures standardised size and quality.

CAM (see page 128)

ON STAGE

enhancement of fabrics

IN YOUR PROJECT

Which of the techniques described on these pages could best be used to decorate the garment you are designing?

Mount all your samples in your design folder in a visually exciting way. Write a short evaluation for each of the samples. Consider the following:
► Has it created the desired effect?
► How difficult was it?
► Did it take a long time?
► What is its creative potential for your project?

KEY POINTS

● Padding and quilting can produce a three-dimensional effect.
● Quilting is a very good way to insulate a garment.
● Very intricate details can be achieved with hand or machine embroidery.
● Some fastenings are decorative as well as functional.

Colouring Fabric (1)

ON STAGE

You can colour your own fabric by using one of the many dyeing and printing techniques which have been developed over the centuries.

Tie and dye, batik and silk painting are resist techniques. Printing techniques include block printing, screen printing and transfer printing. Others involve direct application of the colour using fabric paints, fabric pens and fabric crayons.

Tie and Dye

Tie and dye is one of the oldest methods of dyeing cloth and some of the best examples originate from India, Africa and Japan. Areas of the fabric are tied with thread or string so that when the cloth is immersed in dye, the tightness of the string resists the dye and prevents it from penetrating to the tied areas. This is known as **resist dyeing**.

Modern techniques for tie and dye are very similar to traditional ones. As well as folding, sewing and binding small objects into the cloth, bulldog clips, staples, pegs and rubber bands are also useful aids.

Tie and dye techniques
First tie up the fabric. Wet the material in clean water and squeeze. Immerse it in the dye and then rinse it thoroughly before untying. Finally leave it to dry. The material can then be re-tied and dyed in a second colour if required.

Tie and dye in Bangladesh

Marbled effect
Crumple up fabric into ball and bind.

Stripes/pleats
Pleat fabric in length and tie at intervals with string or rubber bands.

Circles
Lift pieces of fabric and bind. Can vary in size and spaces between circles.

Square tied patterns
Follow the diagrams for dramatic sunburst effects.

Batik

Batik uses wax to stop dye penetrating the fabric

Silk Painting

Silk painting uses **gutta** (outliner) as a resist.

Silk Georgette by Judy Dwyer

Materials for Dyeing

The natural fibres – wool, cotton, linen and silk – dye extremely well as they are very absorbent. Man-made fibres can be dyed but cplours are generally not as strong as on natural fibres.

The colour of the fabric you start with is very important. If you dye a white fabric blue, it will turn out blue. If you dye a yellow fabric blue it will turn out green. Look at the information about the colour circle on page 28.

Calico

Calico is a fabric you may find useful throughout your project. It is a plain weave cotton cloth which may be bleached or unbleached. Calico can be bought in different weights. Although it does not drape well it is ideal for dying and printing.

Dyes

Japanese herbalists developed a range of natural dyes. One of the most common was indigo which became the Japanese national colour for workwear.

Until the 1850s all dyes were natural in origin. Then a great deal of research into chemical dyestuffs began and the science became highly developed in France, Germany and England.

The **chemical dyes** were so successful that by the beginning of the twentieth century synthetic dyes were used for most of the coloured textiles produced in Europe and America. They have several advantages over natural dyes:

▶ the colours are much brighter and cleaner
▶ they are much cheaper
▶ they are easier to make

▶ because they are made to scientific formulae the same colour can be reproduced again and exactly matched.

Scientists continue to research dye development. Today textile manufacturers have thousands of different colours to choose from.

⚠ SAFETY FIRST!

- Wear an apron and use rubber gloves.
- Mix dyes over newspaper.
- Dyes will stain so make sure you do not splash them onto floors, walls, clothing and skin
- Wash up bowls, brushes, etc., immediately after use.

■ ACTIVITIES

▶ Find out what dyes you have available in school or are available in the shops, such as hot and cold-water dyes, micron dyes and craft dyes.
▶ Produce your own small samples of tie and dye.
▶ Try tie and dyeing an old T-shirt at home.
▶ Other methods of resist dyeing include batik and silk painting. Investigate one of these techniques.
▶ Find out more about making your own dyes from natural sources.

IN YOUR PROJECT

▶ Would tie and dye be a good technique to use to decorate all or part of the garment you are making?
▶ Take colour and pattern symbolism into account.
▶ What embellishment techniques could you combine with Tie and Dye?

KEY POINTS

● Tie and dye is a resist method for dyeing fabric.
● Natural fibres are the best for dyeing as they are very absorbent.
● It is important to think carefully about the colours you use when dyeing.
● The way in which the fabric is tied will affect the final design.

Colouring Fabric (2)

Stencilling

Stencilling is where shapes are cut from a piece of paper. The stencil is placed on the fabric and paint is applied through the cut-outs with a special brush or sponge.

Stencilling is another decorative art form which the Japanese excelled at. The craft reached its peak between 1603 and 1868 (the Tokugawa Shogunate Dynasty) and created the opportunity for people outside the ruling class to wear brightly coloured patterned clothing.

The designs became very complex. Wooden stencils were replaced by layers of paper and they were cut using a wide variety of blades and awls. Sometimes parts of the stencil were held together by a very fine silk thread.

Floral and plant motifs such as irises, cherry blossom, chrysanthemum, maple leaf, bamboo, honeysuckle and various grasses were commonly used to create the pattern and these were often combined with hats, fans, fences, bridges, cranes and waterfowl. These frequently had a symbolic meaning. Many patterns were asymmetrical but classical repeat patterns were also very popular.

You can create stencils in a paint, graphics or CAD program; these can be printed directly onto card or acetate.

You could scan some images from your sketchbook; the ideas can be adapted and simplified for use as a stencil.

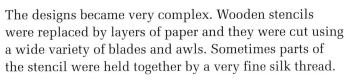

Stencil designs including plum blossom, cloud and mist, hemp leaf and spirals.

■ ACTIVITY

In your project folder design some motifs from which you could make a stencil. Place your motifs inside a square and imagine how you could cut them out. Keep them simple. They can still be very effective if repeated.

Cut out a stencil and try it out on fabric or in your project using paint. Try repeating it in different ways. See how many patterns you can create from one simple motif.

Making a stencil

You will need a natural fibre fabric (plain weave cotton or calico are ideal), fabric paints, a stencil brush or sponge, sticky tape and an iron.

An alternative to the fabric paint is pastel dye sticks. These can be applied like an oil pastel and blended together. They can be embroidered over.

1 Stencils are traditionally cut from waxed paper but you can use thin (preferably clear) plastic or cardboard. Try rubbing a wax candle or clear nail varnish around the cut-out edges in order to make it waterproof. When

transferring your design to the paper, make sure you leave a good sized border around the design so that the paint does not smudge over the edge of the card when applied. Cut out using a craft knife. Protect the surface underneath.

2 Stretch fabric onto surface and hold down with sticky tape. If the fabric is creased iron it first. Mark on the fabric with chalk where you want the stencil to go so that it is positioned correctly. Position stencil and tape if necessary.

3 Apply paint with sponge or brush using an up and down movement only. Paint may slip under the edge of the cut-out if a sideways movement is used. Apply paint sparingly at first and build up colour gradually. Remove stencil carefully, allow to dry and iron on the back to fix colours.

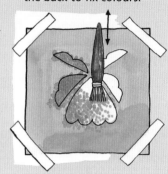

Direct Application

Fabric paints can be applied with a brush to create large background areas and/or a solid effect.

Applying fabric paint with a sponge will create a textured effect. Let the first colour dry and apply a second to give added depth to your design.

Fabric crayons can give you bold lines or try using them on their side to give a textured effect and try using more than one colour. They can also be used instead of fabric paint to create your stencil design.

Fabric pens are excellent for adding clearly defined lines and fine details.

Remember to heat-set the colours when they have dried to prevent running and smudging.

■ ACTIVITY

Use coloured pencils, pens and wax crayons to create some direct application designs in your folder. This should be fun since the limitations are fewer than for other techniques. Try one out on a small piece of fabric.

IN YOUR PROJECT

▶ Mount all your samples in your project, including the stencils you used, label and evaluate.

▶ How effective are these techniques? Could you use them for your costume?

▶ Is it possible to combine any of the colouring techniques in one design? Which ones could you use in combination with the embellishment techniques?

KEY POINTS

● Designs for stencilling can be complex.

● Stencils enable you to repeat a design over and over again.

● Stencils allow you to build up a detailed pattern from a simple motif.

ON STAGE

enhancement of fabrics

Adapting a Pattern

ON STAGE

Patterns are used to create three-dimensional structures from material. Existing patterns can be adapted or new ones created. Conventional methods of marking up the pattern need to be used, so everyone can follow them.

What is a Pattern?

Making a **pattern** allows you to alter a piece of flat fabric into a three-dimensional structure for a human being.

There are several ways to approach pattern making.

Block pattern

A **block pattern** is a foundation pattern constructed to fit an average figure. In industry there is a standard block pattern for every size of a particular garment. The pattern-cutter will adapt the standard block to create the style and fashion details required by the designer.

Commercial patterns

For home dressmaking you can buy **commercial patterns** which have already been adapted to create a particular style. In school you may have some block patterns or commercial patterns but they may not be the right shape, so you may need to alter them in various ways to suit your design.

SIZE SYMBOL	8	10	12	14	16	18
HORIZONTAL MEASUREMENTS						
BUST	80	84	88	92	97	102
WAIST	58	62	66	70	75	80
HIPS	85	89	93	97	102	107
BACK WIDTH	32.4	33.4	34.4	35.4	36.6	37.8
CHEST	29.8	31.2	32.6	34	35.8	37.6
SHOULDER	11.75	12	12.25	12.5	12.8	13.1
NECK WIDTH	6.75	7	7.25	7.5	7.8	8.1
DART	5.8	6.4	7	7.6	8.2	8.8
ARMHOLE	37.5	39	40.5	42	43.5	45
VERTICAL MEASUREMENTS						
NAPE TO WAIST	38.5	39	39.5	40	40.5	41
SHOULDER TO WAIST	38.5	39	39.95	40.2	40.9	41.6
ARMHOLE DEPTH	20	20.5	21	21.5	22	22.5
WAIST TO KNEE	56	57	58	59	59.5	60
WAIST TO HIP	21	21..25	21.5	21.75	22	22.25
SLEEVE MEASUREMENTS						
LENGTH TO WRIST	55.75	56.5	57.25	58	58.5	59
TOP ARM	24.8	26.2	27.6	29	30.5	32
WRIST	15	15.5	16	16.5	17	17.5
MEASUREMENTS FOR PANTS						
BODY RISE	26.5	27	27.5	28	28.5	29
SIDE SEAM	101	102	103	104	104.5	105
FINAL KNEE WIDTH	25.8	26.4	27	27.76	28.4	29.2
FINAL HEM WIDTH	25.8	26.4	27	27.6	28.4	29.2

Copying

Find a garment at home which resembles the size and shape of your design, for example dressing gowns and T-shirts are often simple T shapes. You could then measure the garment and make your own pattern.

Remember – do not throw your pattern away. Keep it in an envelope, mounted in your project folder.

IN YOUR PROJECT

▶ Explore the different ways you could make your pattern, icluding ICT.
▶ Ask your teacher whether there are block patterns available in school or whether you will have to adapt a commercial pattern. Show the adaptations necessary in your folder.
▶ Make a scale model in paper.
▶ After experimenting draft your own pattern.

Modelling

▷ Make a model the right size out of newspaper. When correct draw each piece out on pattern paper.

▷ For a very complex design, designers often make up a muslin or calico sample of the garment (called a **toile**) first. For a theatrical costume the actor playing the part can try it on so that the fit can be examined and adjustments made if necessary. This allows the designer to check the design before good quality fabric is cut.

▷ Try making a miniature model from scrap paper. Roughly sketch the pattern pieces you will need for your design and then make a miniature out of scrap material. This will show you which pieces should be the same length – for example back side-seams should be the same length as front side-seams – and in which order tasks have to be carried out.

The traditional Japanese **kimono** was a very simple T-shaped garment with no pleats or darts. Although the decoration was often highly complex, the construction was simple.

A kimono is made from a set length of fabric called a tan. Kimonos were worn layer upon layer and women's often had extra material on the front sides and a neckband.

Adapting a Block Pattern

To alter a block or commercial pattern you will have to do the following:

1 Make a note of all the measurements you will need for your pattern. You could work in pairs to do this. Use the diagram as a guide to which measurements you will need.

2 Look at the blocks or commercial patterns available to you and decide which pieces you need. Make a large clear diagram of them in your project folder.

3 Use a different coloured pen or pencil and mark the alterations you will need to make on the diagram. You might need to alter any of the following – length, width, armhole length, sleeve length.

Block pattern for a simple T-shirt garment

Alterations for a simple T-shirt garment

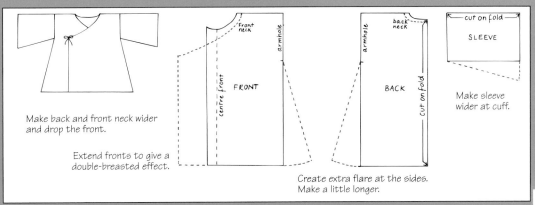

Make back and front neck wider and drop the front.

Extend fronts to give a double-breasted effect.

Create extra flare at the sides. Make a little longer.

Make sleeve wider at cuff.

4 You now need to add **pattern markings**. Use the diagram as a guide.
Seam allowances may be included on the block you used. If not you must add them as they will allow you to sew together your garments to the original size intended. A 10 mm seam allowance is used in industry. Commercial patterns usually have a seam allowance of 15 mm.
Pattern piece = size of intended finished garment + 10 millimetre seam allowance.

5 Now you are ready to draw out the pattern on **pattern paper** using the correct measurements. Follow the same procedure you have followed in your folder. Start by drawing round the blocks on pattern paper.

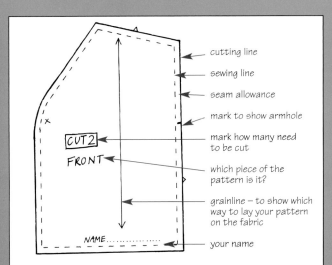

— cutting line
— sewing line
— seam allowance
— mark to show armhole
— mark how many need to be cut
— which piece of the pattern is it?
— grainline – to show which way to lay your pattern on the fabric
— your name

KEY POINTS

- A pattern will enable you to create a three-dimensional structure from a piece of flat material.
- Patterns can be adapted to create different styles.
- There are various ways to make your own pattern.
- Patterns must always have pattern markings and seam allowances.
- In industry ICT is used to create layplans and patterns.

ON STAGE

modelling

Cutting it Out

When you have completed your pattern you are ready to cut it out. Before doing this there are some things you should know about fabrics.

Grainline

The **grainline** on the pattern shows you which direction to lay your pattern piece on the fabric.

Garments are normally cut on the lengthwise grain. This is very important as a garment not cut on the straight grain will not hang properly because fabric cut on the **bias** behaves differently.

Selvedges – the edges of the roll which have been finished off by the manufacturer.

Grain lines – the weave of the fabric which is parallel to the selvedge. The straight grain can also follow the weft threads.

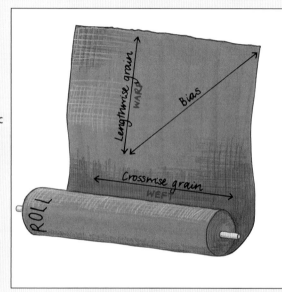

Warp – threads which run parallel to the selvedge.

Weft – threads which run at right angles to the warp thread.

Bias – cuts across the warp and weft threads.

■ ACTIVITY

1. Get a piece of fabric and pull it across the lengthwise grain and the crosswise grain.
▶ How does it behave?
▶ Does it stretch?

Now pull it across the bias.
▶ Does it behave differently?

2. Find out about fabrics with a **nap** or **pile**. What are they? What must you consider when cutting out a garment from a fabric which has a nap or pile?

3. What additional care is necessary when cutting out garments from fabric which has stripes, checks, large motifs or a pattern with a one-way print? Write up the results of your research in your fabric swatch book.

Detail from silk satin evening dress by Christian Lacroix, 1988

Pattern Lays

You must now place your pattern pieces on your chosen fabric in such a way that as little fabric as possible is wasted. You may need to iron the fabric and/or pattern first. Consider the following:

▷ Each piece is usually cut on the double because either it is a half-piece such as the back or because two pieces are needed (e.g. sleeves).

▷ When only one piece is needed it should be cut on single material (e.g. waistband).

Position the largest pieces first and then fit the smaller pieces around them. Pieces should be as close together as possible. There does not need to be any space between them at all. In industry this is very important as a saving of a few centimetres of fabric can reduce the total cost of a garment considerably.

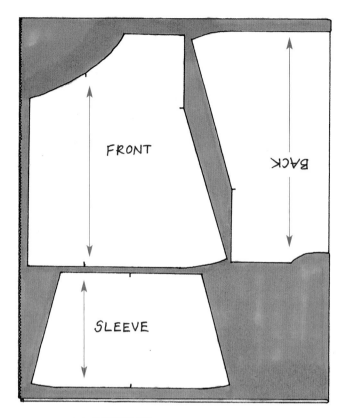

■ ACTIVITY

Experiment by arranging your pattern pieces on your chosen fabric until you find the most economical lay. Fabric comes in standard widths e.g. 115 cm and 140 cm. Which width do you think would give you the most economical lay?

To find out more about industrial pattern making go to:
www.gerbertechnology.com
www.lectra.com
www.assyst-intl.com
www.padsystems.com

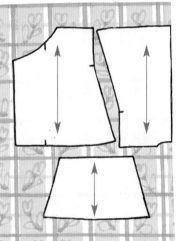

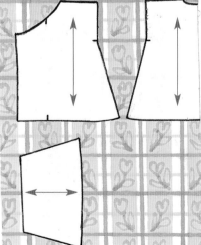

IN YOUR PROJECT

▶ Draw a diagram of the final lay for your garment

KEY POINTS

● It is important to understand what the warp, weft and bias are when working with fabrics.

● The grainline on a pattern shows you which way to position the pattern piece on the fabric.

● A pattern lay is positioning your pattern pieces on your fabric in as economical a way as possible.

Putting it Together

ON STAGE

You need to prepare properly before starting to construct your design. There are many technical considerations such as choosing the correct needle and thread and ensuring you know how to use the sewing machine properly to construct even seams that will not fall apart.

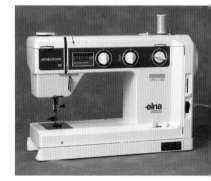

The construction of theatrical garments can be quite different from the construction of everyday garments.

▷ The construction should be able to withstand quick changes between scenes.

▷ The garment may have to withstand a certain amount of wear and tear on stage depending on the part played by the wearer. Seams should therefore be very secure. The stitches should be checked frequently and a reverse stitch should be used at the beginning and end of every seam.

▷ There is no need to overlock or finish edges unless the fabric frays a lot.

▷ Seams should be pressed open and flat as you go along – this will enhance the finished quality of the garment.

▷ Zig-zag seams should be used to join knit fabrics to allow for give.

▷ Machine hems where possible.

■ ACTIVITIES

1. Revise how you use the **sewing machine**. In your project folder write down what the following are for:

▶ balance wheel
▶ presser foot
▶ feed dog
▶ foot pedal.

Thread your machine up and set it on a straight stitch. Practice sewing on a piece of scrap fabric. Try out some different stitches.

2. Re-set your machine on straight stitch. Cut two pieces of fabric to the same size and join them together using a plain seam with reverse as shown in the diagrams on page 45.

Refer to the charts below to make sure you are using the right needle, thread, and stitch length and width.

3. Mount your test pieces in your project folder and explain what the reverse stitches are for.

4. Make a flow diagram of the construction of your garment. Use the diagrams on the next page to help you.

What machine needle should you use?

Fabric	Needle size	Needle type
Lightweight-cotton lawn, silk, lace	11 (80 metric size)	Sharp point
Medium weight – polycottons, cottons, e.g. needlecord, poplin, and prints	14 (90 metric size)	Sharp point
Heavyweight – woollens, cottons, e.g. corduroy, velvet, terry-towelling, gabardine	16 (100 metric size)	Sharp point
All knitted fabrics	According to weight	Ball point

Your thread should match the fabric in thickness and fibre type.

Getting it stitched up
Here is a rough guide to help you work out what stitch length, stitch width and needle position you need:

	Stitch length (mm)	Stitch width (mm)	Needle position
Straight stitch	2 ½	0	Centre
Gathering	4	0	Centre
Zig-zag	2	3-4	Centre

The finer the fabric the shorter the stitch e.g.
▶ For acetate lining – 2mm
▶ For medium weight – 3mm
▶ For quilting and thicker fabric – 4mm +

Constructing a seam

1 Pin two pieces of fabric together.

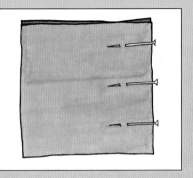

2 Use the marked guidelines on the machine to sew down line with machine and reverse at each end.

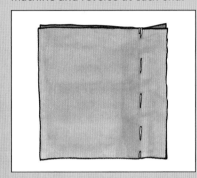

3 Press the seam open and flat with an iron.

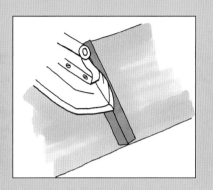

Final construction

1 Apply stencil designs to the back and front of the garment. Allow to dry. Press the back with an iron in order to fix the colour.

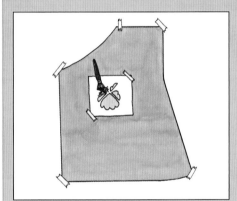

2 Join front shoulders to back. Remember to put right sides together.

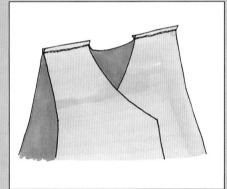

3 Press open shoulder seams with an iron.
Stitch sleeves to garment before side seams and sleeve seams are stitched. Close garment right sides together and stitch sleeve and side seam.

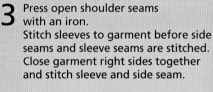
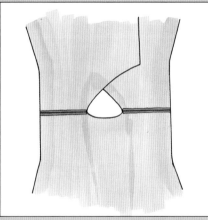

4 Hem edges twice. Press up and stitch on the machine – cuffs, fronts, back neck and around the bottom.

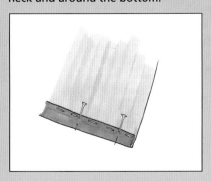

5 Turn right side out. Pin, tack and sew on trim around the edges.

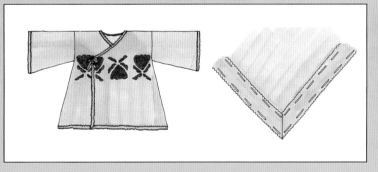

Planning the Making/Testing and Evaluating

You will be presenting your ideas at a production meeting at which the theatre director and other people involved in the production will be present. Some careful planning and preparation will be needed to ensure you have all of the following ready on time:

▷ *initial ideas for costumes or stage set fabrics*

▷ *test pieces*

▷ *a sample costume for one of the main characters, or samples of fabrics for the stage set*

▷ *ideas for the stage set.*

Planning Check-list

▷ Time: how long will each task take? Which task do you think will take the longest? How much time do you have to complete the garment?

▷ Will you be able to obtain appropriate materials in time?

▷ What tools and equipment will you need?

▷ How can you minimise waste of time and materials?

▷ How can you ensure that your finished garment is of a good quality?

Have you practised all the techniques you are going to need? If not it is a good idea to do so as this will enhance the quality of the final item.

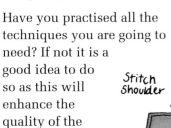

Time Management

You must be aware of how long it is taking you to complete each task and how long you have left. You may have over or under-estimated the time available, in which case you may have to adjust your plan or your final design.

Quality Control

In industry there is always a system of **quality control**. This involves checking the quality of the item being made at various stages of its production.

A series of quality specifications, which include tolerance levels, must be produced. These inform how exactly the job should be done and provide the Quality Controller with something against which to check an operation is working.

It is a good idea for you to check your making as you go along and record it alongside your production plan.

Week	Activity	Tools/ Equipment	Quality control
1	Cut out Prepare stencils	Scissors, tailors chalk, paper, craft knife, pencil	Found it difficult to keep the fabric flat when pinning
2	Apply stencil designs to garment pieces. Iron back to fix colours	Tape, stencils, clean surface, sponges, brushes, fabric paints	
3	Join front shoulders to back and press open and flat.		

Final Testing

You could test each other's work by holding your own production meetings in class in groups of four or five. Present your work to the group and discuss your ideas with them. The outcomes of the meeting need to be recorded in some way. Try drawing up a chart similar to the one shown in which comments and ideas can be recorded.

Remember to make positive comments about each others work and suggest constructive improvements.

Criteria	Make comments on
Interpretation of the theme	Your overall view of the entire project. • How strong is the Japanese theme and is it consistent throughout the project? • How would it appear during a performance of The Mikado?
Colour ideas and co-ordination	Are they appropriate for the theme? • Do colours chosen for costumes reflect the characters? • Do colours for sets create the right atmosphere?
Initial ideas for costumes or fabrics for the stage set	Overall use of shape, style, colour, etc. • What will they look like from a distance when on stage? • Are they appropriate for the atmosphere of the musical and the character?
Test pieces	Overall use of colour, design, etc. • Could any of the colours/techniques be developed more for the final designs?
Sample costume or fabrics	Overall colour, shape, style, details and techniques. • What will it look like on stage with the sets. • Are they appropriate for the theme and the storyline? • Do they create the right atmosphere?

Turning Japanese ?

Perhaps the most memorable part of last night's opening night of a new production of *The Mikado* was the stunning costumes and stage-set. A dazzling spectacle of rich, vivid purple and gold costumes and fabric screens derived from traditional Japanese patterns and motifs instantly transported the audience into nineteenth century Japan.

The final test – what the theatre critics say...!

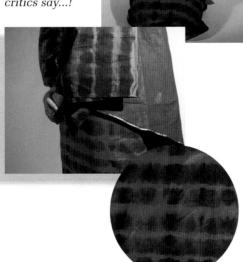

Final Evaluation

Check your work against the requirements of the original specification, e.g. in terms of the function, aesthetics, safety, cost and materials.

Assess the quality of design (i.e. the use of theme, colour, shape, style, pattern) and the quality of manufacture (i.e. the finishing off of seams, top-stitching, techniques, dyeing/painting, etc.).

Make sure you write up your final evaluation in your design folder.

KEY POINTS

● Planning the production of your product is very important.
● Thorough planning will lead to a 'quality' product.
● Considering time limitations is necessary if you are to complete your project successfully.

ON STAGE

realisation

Examination Questions

You should spend about one and a half hours answering the following questions. To complete the paper you will need some plain A4 and A3 paper, basic drawing equipment, and colouring materials. You are reminded of the need for good English and clear presentation in your answers.

Before attempting the following questions you will need to do some preliminary research into:

● images and fashions associated with the 1960s
● how colour and texture can be used to create interesting effects.

Design Brief

A national art centre is hosting an exhibition of 1960s fashions and wishes to sell souvenir products in its craft shop. The exhibition will be open for twelve months and it is expected that many visitors will want to buy the products.

Your client, the craft shop buyer, has asked you to design one of the following:

1. A range of fashion accessories.
2. A range of cushions.

The products are to:

● use the theme of 'black and white' in an exciting and original way.
● be embellished using a method which gives a textured effect.

You must choose either 1. or 2. and then relate all your answers to the following questions to the product range you have selected.

1. **This question is about research for your product range.** *(Total 15 marks).* See pages 6-11.

(a) Give three sources of inspiration for the black and white theme. *(3 marks)*

(b) The theme has been used many times in relation to the 1960s.

   (i) Give two advantages of working to a well-used theme. *(2 marks)*

   (ii) Explain how you will make sure your designs are fresh and appeal to consumers of the twenty-first century. *(4 marks)*

(c) Write down three things that might affect the sort of designs you produce. Give a reason why you think that each factor is important. *(6 marks)*

2. **This question is about the design of your product range.** *(Total 35 marks).* See pages 12-13, 20-21, 30-31.

(a) The specification for the products states that they:

● are to use the theme of 'black and white' in an exciting and original way.
● are to be embellished using a method which gives a textured effect.
● are to have a fastening

(i) Sketch initial ideas for two different products using the specification given. One of these ideas is to be developed into a final design. *(6 marks)*

(ii) Choose one of your ideas for development. Give two reasons why you have chosen this design. *(2 marks)*

(iii) Explain two points to be considered when choosing the fastening. *(4 marks)*

(b) Using sketches, labelling and notes, present a final design for your product. Show how you intend to use embellishment to give a textured decorative effect.

Marks will be awarded for:

- the textured decorative effect *(4 marks)*
- originality and inventiveness of the design *(3 marks)*
- the fastening *(2 marks)*
- form, function and quality of the design *(6 marks)*

(c) You will need to present your product ideas to the client.

(i) Describe what you would put in a presentation report. *(3 marks)*

(ii) Explain how you could use information and communication technology (ICT) in this presentation. *(5 marks)*

3. **This question is about the embellishment of the fabric.** *(Total 14 marks).* See pages 32-39.

(a) The fabric is to be decorated to give a textured decorative effect. As part of your development work you will need to experiment with techniques to find the best method of achieving this effect.

(i) Write down three things you will need to consider when choosing a technique for the decorative effect. *(3 marks)*

(ii) Name two different techniques which could be used to give texture on the product you have designed. *(2 marks)*

(iii) Which technique would you use for your product? Explain why. *(3 marks)*

(b) Use notes and diagrams to describe how you would work the technique you have chosen.

(6 marks)

4. **This question is about the manufacture of the product you have designed.** *(Total 16 marks).* See pages 40-47.

(a) You will need to make a pattern for your product.

(i) Describe three different ways of doing this. *(6 marks)*

(ii) The pattern you make will need to be tested. Explain why. *(2 marks)*

(b) Quality control is important to ensure a high quality product.

(i) Describe two checks that will be needed at the cutting out stage and explain why they are necessary. *(4 marks)*

(ii) Describe two checks that will be needed when the fastening is applied to the product and explain why they are necessary. *(4 marks)*

Total marks = 80

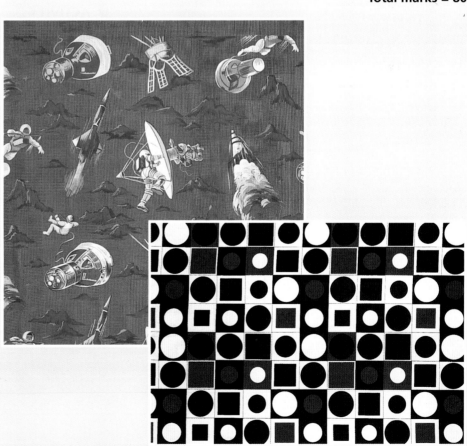

Project Two: Introduction

Textiles play an essential role in the area of sports and leisurewear. As a freelance designer you have been asked by a local company to develop a new range of bags and garments which can be used in very different ways.

Ergonomics
(page 62)

Fabric
Constructions
(page 70)

Construction
Methods
(page 78)

GETout is a well-established company which specialises in the production of garments and accessories for a wide range of outdoor activities such as camping, walking and cycling.

To begin with we planned to revitalise our business by developing a new co-ordinated product range of small containers/bags and outside garments with special pockets for such activities. However our market research has shown that there are new uses for our products within the typical family.

We therefore need to re-think our designs drastically, and need some new ideas to take us forward. We are therefore hoping you will be able to design a highly adaptable bag, rucksack or carrier and/or garment which will appeal to our potential family market.

– 1 –

Clarifying the Brief

Carefully read the letter on the left.

Make a list of all the things the client expects you to do.

Are you going to concentrate on the bag or the garment?

■ ACTIVITY

Start to look through catalogues, magazines and in shops, etc., to find out what type of products are already on the market.

Collect pictures and make sketches. Note down materials and trimmings used and cost.

What we need to see are:

* a statement of the range of different situations in which the bag or garment could be used, and what it will be able to carry.
* sketches to show colour variations and adaptable sections that could be added or taken off according to use
* a prototype model of one container or garment, showing how it can be adapted.
* a name and logo for our new product range to help give it a strong identity in the mind of the public.

Remember that the adaptability of the product is very important, and the key to our success.

I look forward to discussing your ideas with you in the near future.

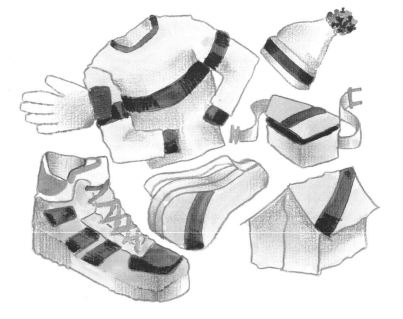

– 2 –

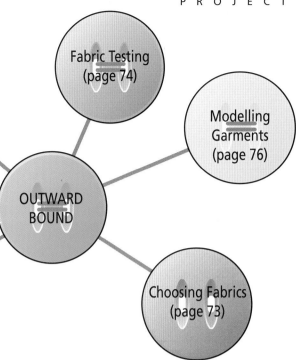

Designing for a Market

Designers must design for people's needs. As different people have different needs designers must have in mind a clearly defined group of people who have similar needs. This group is called a **target market**.

Some target markets may be very broad, such as adults aged 25-40 years, or they may be quite small, such as very young children with specific disabilities.

GETout's research helped them build up the following picture of their target market, which proved to be very broad.

MARKET RESEARCH PROFILE

*The GETout Family
are Outward Bound...*

Dad has developed an interest in mountain biking and photography while Mum wants something to take her kit in for her T'ai chi course every Thursday evening.

Sarah, who insists on being known as Serena, is in her mid teens and needs a bag for a disco sleep-over, which will hold just about anything (and she's not saying what).

Meanwhile Brian, her older teenager brother wants to GETout to a rock concert at Hestonbury, and needs something to store everything he'll need to survive for three days.

They also need some outdoor wear which will keep them warm and dry, and will help them carry the various things they need. Again something that Mum and Dad can share, or Serena and Brian can fight over whose turn it is to use, would be ideal!

Look at the websites of leading designers and brands of clothing.
To find out more about target audiences and trends go to:
www.etexx.com
www.wgsn.com
www.mintel.com

KEY POINTS

- Designers design for a specific group of people called a target market.
- To find out about a market, designers and manufacturers often carry out market research.

Carry on Carrying

There is a limit to how much our hands and arms can hold. People have always used their ingenuity to find better and easier ways of carrying things.

What different ways can you think of for transporting your possessions, safely and comfortably?

How often have you tried to carry a lot of small objects around at once, only to discover you keep dropping things? There are a wide variety of bags, boxes and other containers that can help make it easier to carry things around.

■ ACTIVITY

Study the containers on this page.
► What things is each normally used to carry?
► What completely different things could they hold?
► When might someone need to use each container?
► What materials might each container be made from?

Manual transport in Kenya

Backpack with headband in Nepal

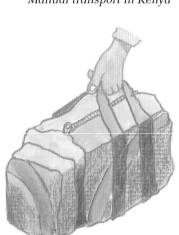

First Thoughts

▷ How many outward bound activities can you think of?

▷ What do people need to carry with them when participating in these activities? Which of these items do you consider to be really vital?

▷ What kind of clothes would they wear?

▷ What sort of image do these activities have?

▷ Do you know any shops or well-known companies which specialise in this area?

▷ How might one basic design be adapted to make it suitable for different uses?

In your design folder, brainstorm your initial thoughts and ideas.

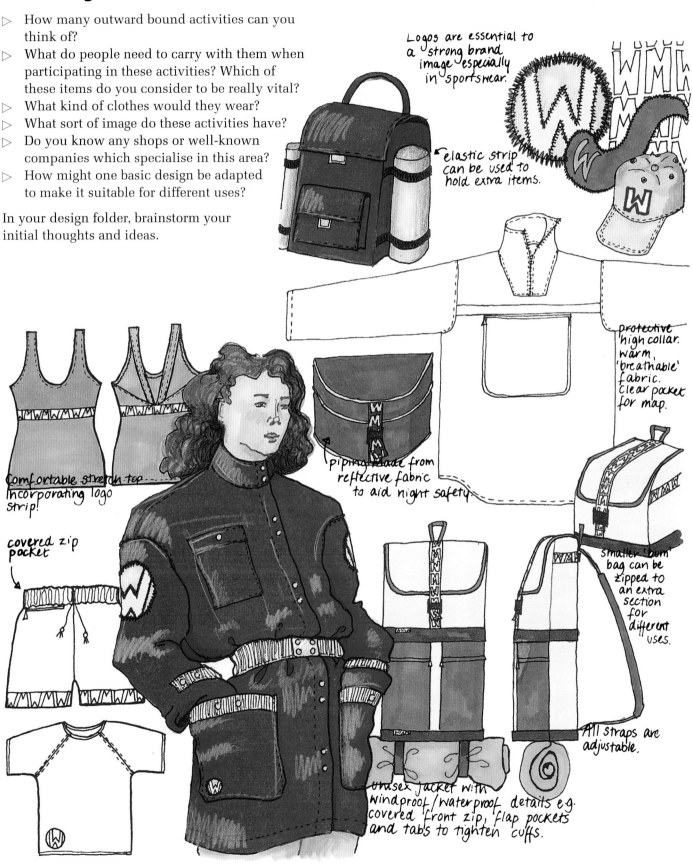

Logos are essential to a strong brand image especially in sportswear.

elastic strip can be used to hold extra items.

protective high collar. warm, 'breathable' fabric. Clear pocket for map.

piping made from reflective fabric to aid night safety

Comfortable stretch top incorporating logo strip!

covered zip pocket

smaller 'bum' bag can be zipped to an extra section for different uses.

All straps are adjustable.

unisex jacket with windproof/waterproof details e.g. covered front zip, flap pockets and tabs to tighten cuffs.

Ergonomic Investigation

You will need to carry out some detailed research into the various elements of your project. You will need to find out more about the ergonomic requirements of your product and target market. Evaluating an existing product will help you understand a lot more about what the problems are.

Ergonomics

Ergonomics is the study of the way in which a product, the user and the environment affect each other. Examples of designs which have not taken ergonomic considerations into account are a jacket for mountain climbing which will not provide protection against very bad weather and a rucksack which is difficult to put on and take off.

Make sure you think carefully about the health, safety, convenience and comfort of the user when analysing, evaluating or developing design ideas.

■ ACTIVITY

Make an ergonomic study of someone you know either trying to carry a number of items in a rucksack or trying to put on or take off a garment which is complicated to do up.

You will need to take some overall measurements of the person and the product, watch them use it and ask them some questions.

▶ Are their arms long enough?
▶ Are their hands big enough?
▶ Can they pick up and carry the loaded rucksack with ease?
▶ Are any pockets easy to open and close? Are they too big or small?
▶ Are any straps long and wide enough, and easy to adjust?
▶ Is it easy to clean and mantain?
▶ Does the user like the colours, shapes, patterns and textures?
▶ Do they enjoy using it?

Product Analysis

Find some different types of containers or garments and make sketches of them in your project folder – back, front and sides. Examine the insides for extra compartments. Enlarge some of the finer details if necessary, e.g. fastenings, logos, decorative stitching, etc.

Alternatively, disassemble an appropriate garment. Examine it carefully and draw diagrams of all the pattern pieces needed to make it. Consider how well it performs in terms of use, safety, adjustability and weatherproofness.

Your conclusions will need to focus on the following questions.

▷ Do you think it is a successful design? Is it fit for its intended purpose?
▷ What are its good and bad points?
▷ Is it ergonomically sound?
▷ Can you suggest any improvements?

Safety

The design of a rucksack must be considered carefully to ensure the well-being and safety of the wearer.

Most of the weight is concentrated on the hips but a certain amount has to be carried through the shoulder straps in order to hold the pack next to the back for stability. This keeps the weight as close as possible to the centre of gravity, otherwise the wearer could easily topple over.

Cyclops Back System

Extendible lid strap

Top tension strap

Top tension adjusters

Ventilation channel

Compression strap sewn right through the frame

Advent fabric for comfort against skin

Windclips to stop excess straps flapping in wind (not visible)

Polypex reinforced hipbelt sewen through the frame

Cynch straps for stability at base

Dual adjust bergbuckle (alloys positioning in either direction)

Adjustability

The distance from shoulders to hips varies from person to person. To ensure that a rucksack fits the back as snugly as possible the back-straps are usually adjustable in length. This means that it can be altered:

▷ to fit a growing body
▷ to fit people of different sizes
▷ to allow for different types of clothing worn in the summer and winter.

Fixed length rucksacks have appeal to some people because of their stability, strength and ease of fit.

Against the elements

How do you make something waterproof? Is using waterproof fabric enough?

▷ Which fastenings are waterproof?
▷ Which designs are most likely to keep out water?
▷ Where is the best place to put seams and fastenings?
▷ How could you make the design more waterproof?

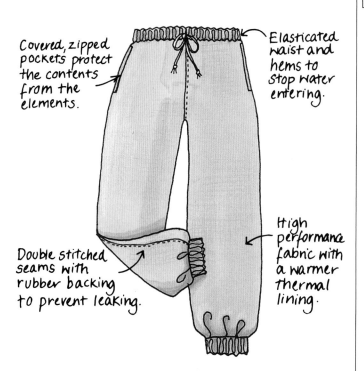

Covered, zipped pockets protect the contents from the elements.

Elasticated waist and hems to stop water entering.

Double stitched seams with rubber backing to prevent leaking.

High performance fabric with a warmer thermal lining.

PRODUCT ANALYSIS CHECKLIST

✔ Describe the sort of person who might wear/carry it and on what sort of occasion.
✔ Where are the seams, top stitching, openings?
✔ Describe the fibres and fabrics used. How might they have been printed or dyed?
✔ Have any trimmings been used effectively?
✔ Have any fastenings been well chosen and placed?
✔ Have any other materials been used, particularly on the inside? If so, why, and how effectively?
✔ Where are the labels and what information is on them? Do they provide enough information?
✔ Is there a brand name or a manufacturer's name?

Fibres to Fabrics

Textile and clothing designers need to have a wider knowledge and understanding of different fibres and fabrics and how they are constructed.

To find out more about fibres, go to:

www.cottoninc.com
www.newzealandwool.com

Fibres to Fabrics

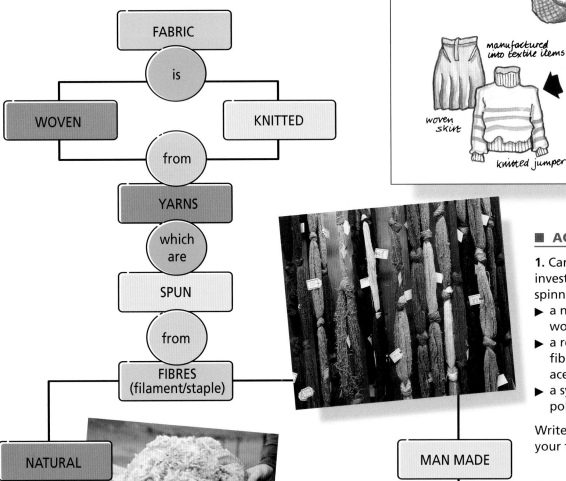

FABRIC

is

WOVEN   KNITTED

from

YARNS

which are

SPUN

from

FIBRES
(filament/staple)

NATURAL   MAN MADE

Animals

silk - worms
wool - sheep

cotton - plant
linen - flax

Plants

cellulose - Viscose
wood pulp - Acetate

Regenerated Cellulose

oil and coal - Nylon
compounds
obtained - Polyester
from coal
oil - Acrylic

Synthetic

woollen fibres taken from sheep

spun into yarns

made into fabric

manufactured into textile items

woven skirt

knitted jumper

woven   knitted

■ ACTIVITIES

1. Carry out an investigation into the spinning process for:
► a natural fibre such as wool or cotton
► a regenerated cellulose fibre such as viscose or acetate
► a synthetic fibre such as polyester or acrylic.

Write up your findings in your fabric swatch book.

2. How many items can you find at home and at school that have been made from cotton? List them in your fabric swatch book and describe the characteristics of the cotton fabric used for each.

Make similar notes for other fibres such as polyester, wool, acrylic and nylon.

The Properties of Fibres

The way a fibre is made into a yarn or the yarn is made into a fabric will affect the final properties of the fabric. For example:

▷ The thickness or weight of a fabric can be altered by using different thicknesses of yarn.

▷ The final texture of a fabric can be altered by adding texture to the yarns it is made from.

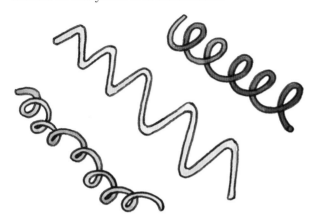

There are many different weaves used to make fabrics, e.g.:

▷ twill weave used to make denim.

▷ pile weave used to make corduroy and velvet.

The way in which a fabric is constructed will affect its properties.

A knitted structure will usually give fabric different properties to a woven one.

Further properties can be given to a fabric by adding different finishes, for example waterproof finish.

Fabrics may therefore have different properties even though they have the same fibre content.

Yarns

Yarns can be made from staple fibres which are short and twisted together to form a yarn or they can be made from filament fibres which are already long and ready for twisting. All natural fibres are staple apart from silk. Silk is the only natural filament yarn: the rest are man-made.

Fibre property chart

A fibre property chart provides a general guide to fabric properties.

	natural fibres				man-made fibres				
	Silk	Wool	Linen	Cotton	Acetate	Acrylic	Nylon	Polyester	Viscose
Abrasion resistance	✻✻	✻✻	✻✻	✻✻	✻	✻✻	✻✻✻	✻✻✻	✻
Absorbency	✻✻✻	✻✻✻	✻✻	✻✻	✻✻	✻			✻✻✻
Elasticity	✻✻	✻✻✻			✻✻	✻✻	✻✻✻	✻✻✻	✻✻
Flame resistance	✻✻✻	✻✻✻	✻	✻	✻	✻	✻✻		✻
Insulation	✻✻✻	✻✻✻	✻	✻	✻✻	✻✻	✻✻	✻✻	✻✻
Mothproof	✻✻	✻	✻✻✻	✻✻✻	✻✻	✻✻	✻✻	✻✻✻	✻✻✻
Mildew resistance	✻	✻	✻	✻	✻✻✻	✻✻✻		✻✻✻	
Resistance to acids	✻	✻✻	✻✻	✻✻	✻✻✻	✻✻	✻	✻✻✻	✻
Resistance to alkalis	✻	✻✻	✻✻	✻✻✻	✻	✻✻	✻✻	✻✻✻	✻✻✻
Resistance to damage by bleach	✻	✻	✻✻✻	✻✻✻	✻	✻✻	✻✻	✻✻✻	✻
Resistance to damage by sunlight	✻	✻	✻✻	✻✻	✻✻	✻✻✻	✻	✻✻	✻
Static electricity	✻✻✻	✻✻✻	✻✻✻	✻✻✻	✻	✻	✻		✻
Tensile strength	✻✻✻✻	✻	✻✻✻	✻✻✻	✻	✻✻	✻✻✻	✻✻✻	✻✻✻
Thermal conductivity	✻	✻	✻✻✻	✻✻	✻	✻	✻	✻	✻✻
Thermoplasticity	I	I	I	I	✻✻	✻✻	✻✻	✻✻✻	I

IN YOUR PROJECT

▶ Which fibres and fabrics would be most suitable for:
– your container?
– your garment?

▶ Why are they suitable?

KEY POINTS

● Fibres can be natural, regenerated cellulose or synthetic.

● Fibres are spun into yarns.

● Yarns can be given added texture by twisting, crimping and looping.

● Fabric construction methods can affect the appearance, texture and properties of the fabric.

● Fabrics can be given special finishes to make them more useful.

OUTWARD BOUND

investigating materials

Specification/Container Design Development

The next stage in developing your designs for GETout is to focus on the possibilities and limitations by preparing a design specification, and then to develop some of your first thoughts into more detailed design ideas.

Review all the information you have gathered during your research and investigation and make the following decisions.

Who is it for?
Make a clear statement of the needs of the people you are designing for.

What will it contain?
List the items it may reasonably need to accommodate.

Materials
What qualities will the materials need to have in terms of strength, durability, weather-proofing, etc.

Size
You can only make an estimate at this stage. Try measuring some of the items that are most likely to be placed in the bag.

Appearance
What sorts of colours, textures and patterns will be most appropriate?

Specification

My container is for...
- It is for carrying...
- It will be no smaller than...
- It will be no bigger than...
- The materials will need to be...
- It must be comfortable to carry and convenient to use, i.e. ergonomically designed
- The shape and colours will....

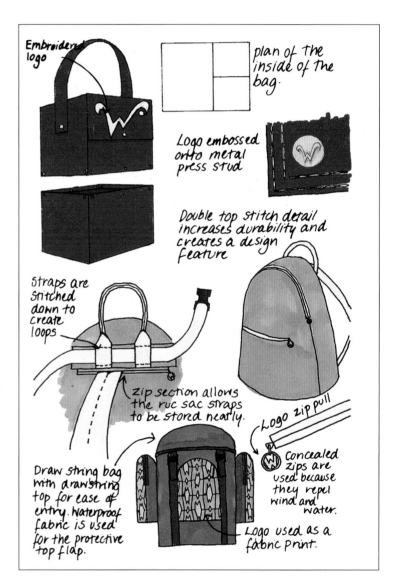

Embroidered logo

plan of the inside of the bag.

Logo embossed onto metal press stud

Double top stitch detail increases durability and creates a design feature

Straps are stitched down to create loops

Zip section allows the ruc sac straps to be stored neatly.

Logo zip pull

Concealed zips are used because they repel wind and water.

Draw string bag with drawstring top for ease of entry. Waterproof fabric is used for the protective top flap.

Logo used as a fabric print.

Developing your Ideas

Read the sections on Fabric Construction and Choosing and Testing Fabrics which follow on pages 70 to 75. You will need to do some of the activities. Make notes in your design folder as your ideas for the GETout bag or garment develop.

As you develop your ideas keep the following questions in mind.

Choosing and testing fabrics

▷ Which **fabrics** will be the most hard-wearing?
▷ Are knitted fabrics as strong as woven ones?
▷ Do you need a fabric which will be able to stretch?
▷ Which will look acceptable to both a teenager and an adult?
▷ Which would make the best combination of style and durability?
▷ What properties will the fabric you choose need to have?
▷ What special finishes could be applied to help make the bag hardwearing and look good at the same time?

Ergonomics

You should also look back at page 62 which asked you to evaluate an existing rucksack from an ergonomic point of view. As you develop your ideas you will need to think about the **ergonomics** of your design. Consider the environment in which your container will be used.

▷ Will it be wet?
▷ Will the user need to carry anything bulky or heavy during the activity?
▷ How many different ways can the container be carried? For example a cyclist will not be able to carry anything by hand or anything very bulky.
▷ How can adjustability be provided?
▷ What methods of carrying would be best?
▷ Which fastenings would be most appropriate?

Detailed Development

After producing some ideas evaluate them. Decide which may be the most promising, and make a note of why.

Develop one or two by focusing on them in more detail. At this next stage features such as size, fastenings and pockets should be considered.

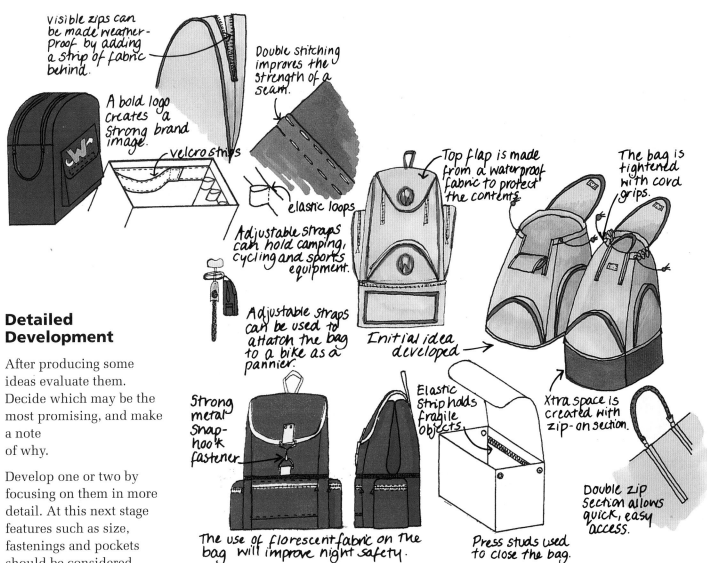

Visible zips can be made weather-proof by adding a strip of fabric behind.

Double stitching improves the strength of a seam.

A bold logo creates a strong brand image.

velcro strips

elastic loops

Adjustable straps can hold camping, cycling and sports equipment.

Adjustable straps can be used to attach the bag to a bike as a pannier.

Strong metal snap-hook fastener

The use of florescent fabric on the bag will improve night safety.

Top flap is made from a waterproof fabric to protect the contents.

Initial idea developed →

Elastic strip holds fragile objects.

Press studs used to close the bag.

The bag is tightened with cord grips.

Xtra space is created with zip-on section.

Double zip section allows quick, easy access.

Specification/Garment Design Development

If you are developing ideas for a garment with special storage pockets to present to GETout, the next stage is to focus on the possibilities and limitations by preparing a design specification, and then to develop some of your first thoughts into more detailed design ideas.

How long do fashions last?

Specification

You need to focus on the possibilities and limitations for your garment by preparing a **design specification**.

The garment will have to be suitable for the activities identified as appropriate to the target market. It will also need to reflect current trends in the use of fabrics, styles and colours for leisurewear.

Review all the information you have gathered during your research and investigation and make the following decisions.

Many sports garments/accessories have become desirable fashion items in themselves. Can you think of any?

Who is it for?
Make a clear statement of the needs of the people you are designing for.

What will it contain?
List the items the wearer may want to carry.

Materials
What qualities will the materials need to have in terms of strength, durability, weather-proofing, etc.

Size
You can only make an estimate at this stage. Try measuring some of the items that are most likely to be placed in it.

Appearance
What sorts of colours, textures and patterns will be most appropriate?

Specification Checklist

- ✔ My garment is for...
- ✔ It is for carrying...
- ✔ The materials will need to be...
- ✔ It must be comfortable to wear and convenient to use.
- ✔ The shape and colours will...

The Influence of Fashion

The market for sports and leisurewear has expanded rapidly in the twentieth century.

Developments in industry and technology have given people more time in which to pursue leisure activities. The market includes all sorts of woven and knitted specialised sportswear and casual garments to suit many different occasions.

Such garments and the accessories that go with them are influenced to some extent by the fashions of the time.

■ ACTIVITY

Carry out an investigation into the growth of the leisure market in this century.
- ► Has the growth of this area affected the way we dress generally?
- ► How has the development of textile technology affected the range of garments on offer to the public? Think about fabric construction as well as fibre development.

Developing Design Ideas

You will need to develop a series of ideas for your garment. Remember that the way it can be adapted to help carry different items must be a key element in the design. Maybe some of your shapes, colours and patterns could be based on ideas taken from historical designs.

If your design is going to be successful you will need to know more about

▷ how fabrics are constructed (see pages 70 to 72)
▷ how to choose the right fabric by analysing its characteristics and properties (see pages 73 to 75).
▷ how to make mock-ups and patterns (see pages 76 to 77).

Presentation

GETout will want to see all your ideas so the way you present your sketches will be very important.

You do not have to be brilliant at drawing people to present garment ideas effectively. You can draw garments and accessories on their own in diagrammatic form.

Experiment to find a way that suits you and enables you to get ideas down on paper quickly and effectively.

You may sketch or trace the outline of a figure from a photograph onto which you can add garments, details and accessories etc. Make yourself a collection of outlines which you can keep in your folder to use.

What are you going to use to render your sketches? Coloured pencils can be very effective. You can also try water-colours, inks and different coloured pens.

■ ACTIVITY

Practise creating textures using different media. Try the following:
▶ rough tweed
▶ satin
▶ woolly jumper
▶ nylon shell suit.

Keeping Warm and Dry

You will need to think about your garment's ability to protect against the elements. Most outdoor jackets attain a high degree of water repellence. Most seams are taped so that they do not leak.

Size
Jackets should be generously sized to allow freedom of movement and allow moisture to evaporate.

Zips
A storm flap, held down by velcro or a press stud will prevent leakage through zip fastenings. Dual zips may be used with a fleece lining to make the garment more versatile.

Length
A longer jacket offers better protection but shorter jackets may be necessary for some active sports.

Hoods
Whether attached, detachable or foldaway they should be large enough to protect against the elements but not restrict vision.

Cuffs
Cuffs should close tightly, using elastic or Velcro to protect against wind and rain

Drawstrings
Drawstrings are usually placed at the hem, waist or hood to stop wind or rain entering. Springlocks make these fastenings easier to use.

Pockets
Pockets may need to be large enough to enable access by someone wearing gloves. Access to some pockets must be possible without undoing the main zip.

An Outfit For The GETout Family

Cotton/viscose mix fabrics are hardwearing and easy to clean

The yolks are made of a printed cotton coated into plastic.

The jacket has a layer of wadding between the outer shell and lining, this helps with warmth.

Embroidered badge

Detachable hood can be stored in zipped section of the collar

Detachable sleeves gives the wearer flexibility

Elasticated cuffs and drawstring hem protect the wearer from the elements

Covered zip pocket

Loose fitting trousers with elastic waistband

Knitted

Herringbone

Woven

Fabric Construction (1)

Most fabrics are constructed by weaving or knitting yarns together. Some are bonded together or felted.

How a fabric behaves depends on the structure of the fabric, the structure of the yarn and the finishes applied.

Get Weaving

Weaving involves the crossing of two sets of **yarns** (the **warp** and the **weft**), over and under each other. Fabrics were traditionally produced on a hand-operated loom. Modern machine operated looms are much more complex and controlled by computer.

Plain weave
A plain weave is the simplest weave: the weft threads pass over and under alternate warp threads. In other weaves the weft is passed over or under more than one warp thread.

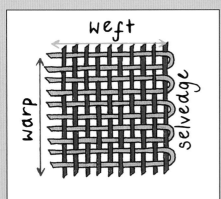

Satin weave
In satin the weft goes under several and over one. Because there is more thread lying on the surface the fabric looks lustrous and glossy.

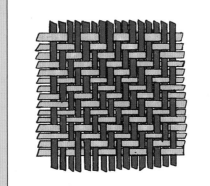

Twill weave
Twill which creates a diagonal pattern on the fabric surface is used to produce strong close weaves such as drill for aprons and overalls and denim used for jeans.

Terry/velvet weave
Some complex weaves such as terry and velvet result in raised or looped surfaces. These are woven by extra warp threads making the loops on a plain weave. The loops increase the surface area of the fabric so that it can absorb more water.

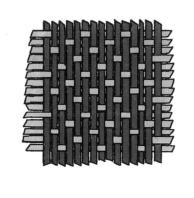

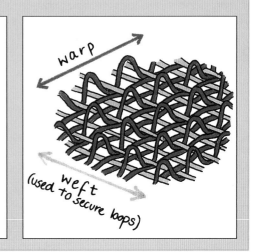

Knitting

Knitting has a looped structure. This is unlike weaving where the yarns remain almost straight.

Weft knitting
The yarn runs across the fabric making loops with the row underneath.

Single jersey
Hand knitters call this stocking stitch (one row plain one row purl). It is often used for T-shirts.

Ribknit or ribbing
Both sides look the same with the ribs of plain and purl running up the fabric. It is very elastic and snaps back into shape very quickly after being stretched. It is used for waistbands, cuffs and neckbands on sweatshirts, tracksuits and woven jackets.

Double jersey
Made on a 'double bed machine' that uses two sets of needles, each with its own supply of yarn. This means that it may be much thicker than single jersey, a firm fabric that lies flat and has much less stretch than single jersey.

Warp knitting
Cannot be produced by hand-knitting like weft fabrics. In warp-knitted fabrics the yarns run 'up' the fabric like the warp yarns in weaving. It can be firm, like a woven fabric or slightly stretchy. It keeps its shape well so it can be used to make very fine, lightweight fabrics and most warp knits do not ladder.

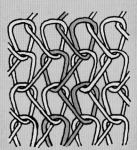

What are the differences between woven and knitted fabrics?
- ▶ Knits have a looped structure and wovens do not.
- ▶ Knits do not fray at the edge the way wovens do although they may run, i.e. the loops may unravel.
- ▶ Knits (particularly wefts) have much more stretch (although wovens have a little more stretch in the bias). Stretch allows us to move with comfort which is why knits are preferred for close fitting casual garments, underwear, tights and sportswear.
- ▶ Knits are usually more open so that air can pass thorough them easily. This is useful on a hot day but not so good on a cold, windy day.

Non-woven Fabrics

Bonded fabrics

Non-woven fabric is generally made from 'webs' or 'batts' of fibre held together and strengthened by bonding. This is achieved by using a resin adhesive, needle-punching, or stitch bonding with thread. The choice is determined by the method of manufacture.

Early non-wovens were unattractive in appearance, handle and drape. It is still difficult to achieve the characteristics of knitted and woven structures. Their advantage is that they are cheaper to manufacture.

As well as being used for interlinings and insulation in clothing, non-wovens are used in disposable hygenic and absorbent products. Other uses include resin-free liners for floppy disks and artificial leathers.

Felting

Felting is an older way of constructing a non-woven fabric. It is made from a combination of moisture, heat, friction and pressure. It is traditionally made from wool but today is more often made from synthetic or recycled yarns. Most carpet underlay is synthetic felt, and it has become popular as a craft material for creative collages and for making hats.

KEY POINTS
- ● Yarns are woven, knitted or bonded into fabrics.
- ● Woven and knit structures give different properties to the final fabric.
- ● Wovens do not stretch as much as knits.
- ● Bonded fabrics can be produced cheaply but are not as strong as woven and knitted fabrics.

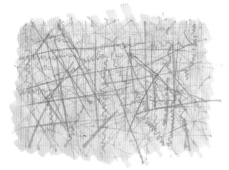

Using adhesive, under pressure and heat, the fibres are bonded together.

Fabric Construction (2)

Something's burning...

Your teacher must supervise you doing the following activity. You will need some fabric samples. Set up a controlled test in which you burn each sample. Use the table below to identify which fibres each is made from.

Disassembly and Evaluation of Fabrics

Investigate some samples of woven, knitted and bonded fabrics. Use a magnifying lens to help you disassemble the fabrics. Record your findings in your fabric swatch book.

▷ Describe the appearance and feel of the sample.
▷ Tease out some of the yarns and examine them. Have they been texturised in any way?
▷ Untwist the yarn carefully. Is it made up of fine fibres? How many fibres make up the yarn? Are the fibres staple or filament?
▷ Is the fabric woven or knitted?
▷ Can you identify the type of weave or knit?
▷ Draw a diagram of the fabric structure

	Burning/flame	Smell	Ash or residue
Cotton/ viscose	Burns readily and quickly Yellow flame	Burning paper	Greyish white ash
Linen	Burns readily Yellowy orange flame	Bonfire smell of burning grass	Grey ash
Wool	Smoulders; burns slowly Fibre burns inside the flame. Does not flare up.	Burning feathers or human hair	Black bead which crushes easily when cold
Silk	Small brittle beads Fibre burns inside the flame. Does not flare up.	Burning feathers or human hair	Burns to ash
Acetate	Slower than viscose	Vinegar smell	Melts to a hard shiny black bead
Nylon	Not flammable i.e. it shrinks away from heat of flame, melting and dripping Yellow flame	Strong celery smell	Light coloured fawn or white hard round bead
Polyester	Difficult to ignite. Melts and shrinks from the flame. Hard beaded edges Luminous red or yellow flame	Strong	Hard round bead, darker than nylon.
Acrylic	Burns then melts Luminous reddish flame	Aromatic odour	Hard black bead of irregular shape

■ ACTIVITY

Carry out an investigation into the fibres and fabrics used for sports and leisurewear and present your findings in a chart as shown below.

Use the properties chart on page 65 and the information on page 71 to say why each fabric was chosen for that particular end use.

Item	Uses	Construction	Fibre content	Reasons for use
Sweat shirt	Casual wear – worn as a tracksuit top	Knitted fabric brushed on one side. Ribbed cuffs	100% cotton	Cotton is soft, comfortable and absorbent – therefore good for sports. Knitted fabric stretches with the body during wear – good for sports. Brushed inside creates extra bulk – traps air, therefore added warmth.

Choosing Fabrics

It is important to choose fabrics which are fit for their intended purpose.

Different fabrics have different properties and characteristics.

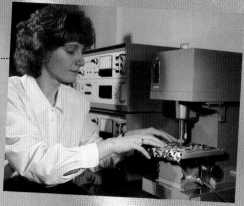

Testing the handle of apparel fabrics

Properties of Fabrics

How will the fabric behave during use?

Abrasion resistance	Windproof	Resilient
Tensile strength	Thermal insulator	Crease-resistant
Washable	Thermal conductor	Non-flammable
Boilable	Absorbent	Thermoplastic
Non-fade	Waterproof	Sunlight resistant
Colour-fast	Showerproof	Mothproof
Non-shrink	Non-irritant	Rot-proof
Drip-dry	Elastic	Resistant to bleach/chemicals

Discuss in groups what the above properties mean.

Characteristics of Fabrics

How will the fabric look, feel, and behave?

Drape	Loosely/tightly made
Thickness	Snagging
Weight	Dimensional stability
Texture	Fraying
Transparency	Hole recovery
Colour and pattern	

Write down all the words you can think of to describe the possible texture of fabrics.

■ ACTIVITY

Undertake some research to discover more about the following finishes:

- ▶ Dry (mechanical) finishing, e.g. Calendering
- ▶ Shrink resist/non-shrink
- ▶ Raising
- ▶ Shearing
- ▶ Wet (chemical) finishing
- ▶ Easy Care finishes
- ▶ Shower-proofing
- ▶ Moth-proofing
- ▶ Anti-static
- ▶ Rubberising

Fabric Finishes

The term finishing covers a wide range of processes which make the fabric suitable for its intended use. It is usually the last stage of fabric processing.

The three basic aims of finishing are:

- ▷ modification of the surface (e.g. raising, smoothing, embossing)
- ▷ modification of wearing properties (staining, creasing)
- ▷ modification of aftercare characteristics (shrinking)

Some finishes such as bleaching are used to improve the appearance of fabrics.

Performance finishes

These are used to give a fabric useful properties or to enhance properties it already has.

Stain and soil resistance

Fabric is finished using a mixture of silicone and fluorine. This prevents grease and dirt entering the fabric which is very useful for carpets and upholstery.

Flame retardance

The flammability performance of fabrics is an essential consideration. The aim is to produce an inexpensive, durable finish which will not compromise handling, strength or wearing properties.

Some finishes work by making the fabric unable to produce fuel vapours that normally feed the flame. Others produce vapours which help suppress the flame. The most widely used finishes are 'Proban' and 'Durovatex'.

Crease resistance

Cotton, linen and rayon crease badly. They can now be treated using a process which involves combining the fibres with a resin. Sometimes, however, this reduces strength and resistance to abrasion.

Modern finishes have greatly improved characteristics. In particular synthetic fibres show very good crease recovery. They are thermoplastic which means they become soft and pliable at higher temperatures. Nylon, polyester and acrylics are thermoplastic. This means that they can be heat-set into shape and given pleats which are permanent.

Brushing

Fabrics can be brushed by passing them through a large rotating brush. This raises the surface of the fabric which means it can trap air and keep the body warmer.

73

Testing Fabrics

Fabrics need to be tested rigorously before a product goes into production to ensure that they will be fit for their intended purpose. There are some simple tests you can do, under supervision, at home or at school. Remember to record your results.

Tensile testing of fabric

Stain Resistance

Stain your fabric with a substance which might be spilt on it during everyday use. Allow it to dry and then try to remove the stain using a method appropriate to the intended use, e.g. tea on upholstery – try removing with a carpet or upholstery cleaner.

Washability

Again stain your fabric samples.

Cut them all to the exact same size so that you can measure them for **shrinkage** after washing. Wash them in a variety of temperatures using the same amount of detergent each time.

Observe and record the following – **stretch**, **shrinkage**, **colour fastness** and **creasing**. Do you think the fabric could withstand frequent washing?

Insulation

Your fabric must be a good insulator if it is to keep you warm.

Fill a glass test-tube with water heated to a set temperature. The test-tube should be fitted with a bung with a hole to insert a thermometer. Retake the temperature after 5-10 minutes and record how much it has dropped. Repeat this test using your fabric wrapped around the tube-test. Also compare the results using different fabrics. Is your fabric the best insulator?

Thermometer
Bung
Test-tube
Heated water
Fabric sample
Rubber band

Stretch and Elasticity

Will your fabric return to its original shape after stretching? Hang strips of fabric, weighted at one end, against graph paper. Make a mark to where the fabric first stretched. Leave for a day and mark again. Remove weights and see if the fabric returns to its original length. You could adapt this experiment to test for **tensile strength**, by using heavier weights.

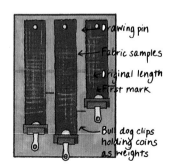

Drawing pin
Fabric samples
Original length
First mark
Bull dog clips holding coins as weights

Abrasion

How hard wearing and durable does your fabric need to be?

Stretch your fabric around a wooden block. Rub with a pumice stone for a given length of time to simulate wear. Which fabric was the most hard wearing?

Absorbency

How much moisture can the fibres of your fabric absorb?

Weigh a range of samples for comparison.

Soak the samples thoroughly and hang them up to dry.

Time how long each one takes to dry.

Waterproofness

How waterproof is your fabric?

Test your fabric by stretching a piece over the top of a jam-jar and spray the top with water. Does any water pass through the fabric into the jar?

Time how long it takes.

Showerproofness

If a fabric is showerproof, water droplets will initially run off the surface, but after a short while start to pass through. Waterproof fabrics will keep moisture out completely. The water will keep running off the surface.

■ ACTIVITY

Discuss the difference between absorbency and waterproofness.

▷ If a fabric is not waterproof is it necessarily absorbent?
▷ Does using waterproof material make a garment waterproof?
▷ What else must you think about when designing such a garment?
▷ What sort of test could be devised for these properties?

Crease Resistance

Crumple your piece of fabric in your hand. Does it crease or does it spring back? Devise a five point scale to compare different fabrics.

Flammability

Burning fabrics needs to be carried out under strict safety conditions. Burn only a small piece of your fabric and use tongs to hold it. Observe and record the following

Tongs
Fabric sample
Candle
Sand box

▷ Is there a flame or does it melt?
▷ Is there smoke or fumes?
▷ Is there a strong smell?
▷ How quickly does it catch on fire and burn?

Refer to page 72 if you need to identify the fibres in the fabric.

IN YOUR PROJECT

▶ It may not be possible for you to obtain a fabric with all the right properties to make your product but you can use a similar one of the right weight for your prototype container.
▶ Record the results of your tests in a table, and draw conclusions.
▶ Discuss the difference between absorbancy and waterproofness. If a fabric is not waterproof is it necessarily absorbent? Does using a waterproof fabric make a garment waterproof?

KEY POINTS

● Different fabrics have different properties and characteristics which make them suitable for different end uses.
● Special finishes can be added to fabrics to give them extra properties.
● Various tests can be carried out on fabrics to find out whether they will be fit for their intended purpose.
● Both fibre content and method of construction affect the final properties of the fabric.

Making, Testing and Evaluating Models

*Making a **model** or **mock-up** of your idea will enable you to see what your final design will look like, and how well it will work.*

*Whether you are making a container or a garment you will need to make up a **paper pattern**.*

ICT

You could use a pattern drafting program to draft out an accurate pattern which you can then print and cut out. It also allows you to quickly try out different layouts.

After developing your design in two dimensions as much as you can you will need to make a model in three dimensions. This has several advantages:

▷ It will give you a much better idea of how your design would look if made from fabric.
▷ It tests whether the design will work by revealing any faults/mistakes at an early stage. This prevents wastage.
▷ Discovering mistakes before a design goes into production saves time and money.
▷ Cheap materials can be used for a model and a very large design can be made on a smaller scale.

You will need paper, scissors, rulers, pens and pencils, sticky tape, and newspaper, scrap paper or card.

The Container

Put the items which your container is designed for inside your model and see if they fit.

▷ Is the shape of your design the right shape for the items? Are the proportions right?
▷ Try the model on someone and assess whether it will be a good design ergonomically.
▷ Do all the pieces fit together properly?
▷ Are the methods of fastening used strong and sturdy enough?

Is there an easier way to construct your design? Make a careful note of all necessary alterations.

Ask others what they think and find out whether it is likely to attract many customers.

Make sure you record your **evaluation** in your design folder.

---

1 Estimate the intended measurements and work out the number of pieces required for your container. Draw a diagram with measurements in rough of each piece.

2 You could try your design out in miniature if your design is on the large side.

3 Measure the pieces out in newspaper and cut out.

4 Now stick your model together. Remember that the order of production is important. Pockets need to be made and attached first.

5 Make a note in your folder of how you make your model. Fastenings can be marked on using felt pens.

CENTRAL PANEL
Cut 1
2·5cm
4·2·5cm

25cm
27·5cm
TOP FLAP
Cut 2

12·5cm
SIDE PANEL
Cut 2
15cm

Experiment with different types of pockets, flaps, fastenings and shapes. How can they best be made inter-changeable?

You could also make up your model using calico. (This is known as 'toile')

The Garment

If you are making a garment, sketch the pattern pieces you will need in your design folder. Work out the correct measurements. You may wish to use a commercial pattern or alter a block pattern (see pages 48 to 49).

Are there any pieces in your pattern which are exactly the same size, e.g. sleeves? If so you will need to make one paper piece and write on it how many times it will need to be cut.

Draw your **pattern** out using the correct measurements on pattern paper and cut out using paper scissors.

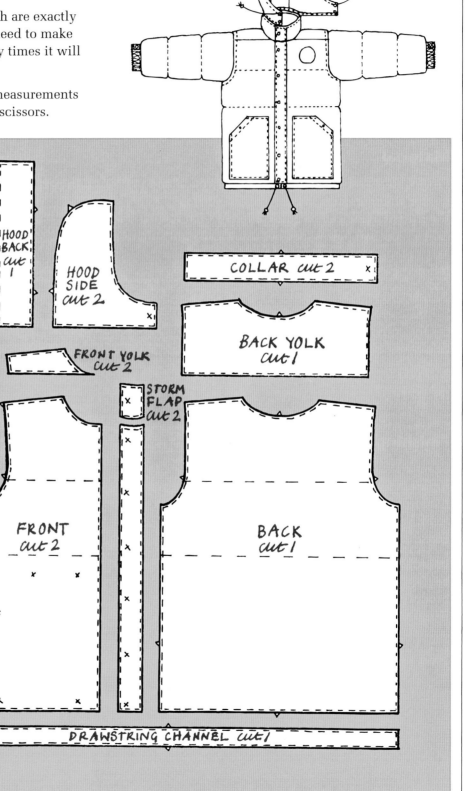

All Stitched Up!

Further knowledge of construction techniques will be needed for you to make your container or garment. You will need to practise finishing edges and adding drawstrings, pockets, etc. If possible use samples of the real material.

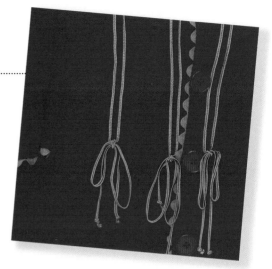

Detail from cotton seersucker mini dress by Mary Quant, 1972.

Material

First of all try **sewing** with the material you intend to use for your container. Sewing fabrics such as waterproof nylon can be quite different from sewing calico. Sew two pieces together using a straight stitch and a plain seam. Experiment until you find the following:

▷ the correct stitch length
▷ the correct needle and thread
▷ the correct tension.

Will you have to tack the fabric together to hold it or will pins be sufficient? Maybe the fabric will stay in position without either.

Finishing Edges

Seam allowances inside the container will need to be finished. Finish both seam allowances together rather than ironing them apart. Try some of the methods on the right. Which will be most appropriate for your construction?

In industry **overlockers** are widely used to finish off edges. They are also used to construct knitwear as they produce a stitch which stretches along with the knitted fabric – an ordinary plain seam cracks when it is stretched. Another alternative is to simply glue back seams rather than stitching them.

▣ ACTIVITY

Look inside some of your own clothes and examine how they have been finished off

Material Specification

In industry a **Material Specification** would be produced. This specifies the most desirable properties and characteristics of the required material as well as what tests might be carried out.

MATERIAL SPECIFICATION		
Essential	**Desirable**	
Waterproof	Washable	
Strong	Stain resistant	
Lightweight		
Good dimensional stability		
Finishes	**Sample**	**Testing**
Showerproof	*(sample of fabric to be used stating fibre content)*	Waterproofness Abrasion Tensile strength

Overlocking
Overlocking is when a seam is stitched and the edges finished in one operation.

Zig-zag
This can be done on an ordinary sewing machine if you do not have an overlocker.

Top-stitching/edge-stitching
This is used on many garments to give a professional finish and add strength. Sometimes it is done in a contrasting colour. It is always found on jeans.

Adding Drawstrings

Make holes for strings first.

Turn down hem twice – once to finish off raw edge and again to make a big enough casing for the cord to go through.

Put edge-stitching around the top to make it more secure.

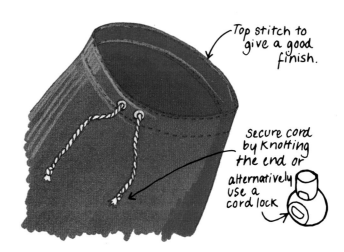

Top stitch to give a good finish.

Secure cord by knotting the end or alternatively use a cord lock

Making Pockets

Two-dimensional pockets
Find out which methods are available to you. Your school may have an overlocker.

Three-dimensional pockets
These pockets can be constructed from separate pieces.

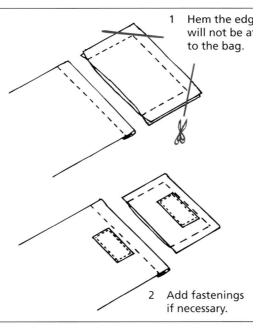

1 Hem the edges which will not be attached to the bag.

2 Add fastenings if necessary.

3 Press in last three edges and stitch to bag. Position and stitch on flap.

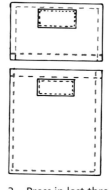

4 Pull flap down and topstitch across the top to make it secure.

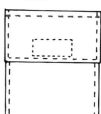

Can you work out how to construct a three-dimensional pocket from one piece of fabric? Try it using paper first.

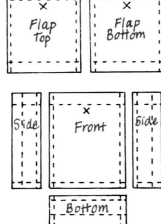

Flap Top

Flap Bottom

Side   Front   Side

Bottom

KEY POINTS

● Different fabrics require different stitch lengths, types of needles and threads, and machine tension.
● Overlockers are widely used in industry to stitch and finish seams.
● Pockets can be made in different ways depending on what type/effect is required.

Consumer Legislation

Over the past thirty years laws have been passed to help protect the consumer from manufacturers who sell shoddy or unsafe goods, or who are dishonest in the claims they make for their product. Some of these laws relate specifically to textile products.

Everyone is a consumer of textile products and services. We all buy, hire or rent a wide variety of clothes and furnishings and often need to have them cleaned, repaired or re-furbished.

There are a number of acts intended to help protect the consumer.

The Trades Descriptions Act

This act means that any claims made about the performance qualities of a product (e.g. easy to wash, hard-wearing) must be true.

Consumer Safety Act

This legislation covers of regulations concerning fire and safety hazards, and includes specifications for items such as children's nightdresses, anoraks and fabric toys. For example, the Nightwear (Safety) Regulations of 1985 insist that thermoplastic sewing threads must be used below the waist or elbow in nightdresses made from thermoplastic material.

■ ACTIVITY

GETout have contacted you to ask what legal requirements their new products will have to conform to. What advice can you give them?

Furniture and Furnishings (Fire Safety) Regulations 1988

These requirements clearly state that such products must be resistant to 'smouldering cigarette ignition'. These requirements cover new and second-hand domestic furniture, cushions, pillows and loose furnishing covers.

The Sale of Goods Act

1. Goods must be of a *satisfactory quality*. They should be durable, safe and have an acceptable appearance. For example, the handle of a new bag should not come off the first time it is used.
2. Goods must be *fit for the purpose* made known to the seller. For example, if a customer has told the shopkeeper they want a warm winter duvet they should not be offered a lightweight summer one.
3. Goods must be *as described*. For example, a leather jacket must be made from leather, and not a synthetic fabric.

Consumer Protection Agencies

There are a number of organisations that have been set up to help protect the consumer. They include:

▷ Local Authority Trading Standards Offices
▷ Local Authority Consumer Protection Departments
▷ The Office of Fair Trading
▷ The Environmental Health Department
▷ The British Standards Institute.

Planning the Making

Making the model should have given you a good idea of how to go about making your design. Make a list of what you will need. Check that everything you intend to use is available, including tools, equipment and materials.

Produce a Production Specification for your final design.

Organise Yourself

Make sure that your workspace is as safe and convenient as possible by planning how you intend to use it. Using the list of items above, draw a plan of your workspace in your project folder. Label where everything should go so that it is as safe and convenient as possible.

Health and safety is very important both in school and in industry. In groups discuss the safety aspects of working with electrical equipment such as sewing machines and irons and list these in your project folder beside your plan.

Finalise the Making Plan

Look back at the rough plan you noted down when making your model. Make any necessary alterations to it.

▷ At which points do you need to finish off edges?
▷ At which points must you add topstitching?
▷ At which point must you add fastenings? It may not be possible to sew velcro to a pocket after it has been stitched to the main structure of the bag.

PRODUCT SPECIFICATION				CONTAINER		
Sketches of front and back view				Fabric and component samples		
				Details of labels and where they should be attached		
DESCRIPTION	SIZE	WORK ORDER	MATERIALS	QUANTITY	COST	
Front length	20cms	1. Make flap	Fabric - Royal	1/2 metre	£3.50 per m.	
Back length	20cms	2. Attach velcro	- Yellow	1/4 metre	£3.50 per m.	
Back width	25cms	3. Make elasticated band				
Front width	30 cms		Webbing - Black	1 1/2 metres		

*In industry a **Product Specification** would be produced. This specifies all the technical details of the making of the product. It communicates to those in charge of production everything they need to know to be able to manufacture the product in bulk.*

Quality Counts

Remember that as your work progresses you will need to check that your work is of an acceptable **quality**. You will need to check:

▷ that the width of the seam allowance is even
▷ that your reverses are no longer than 1 cm
▷ that your overlocking is on the edges and has not missed the fabric or cut through the seam.

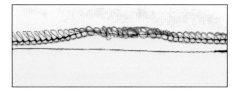

Overlocking has missed edge

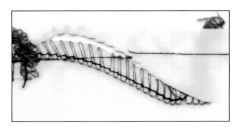

Overlocking has cut into bag

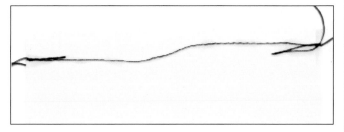

Crooked seam

Untidy reverses

Testing and Evaluating

Your final product must be tested and evaluated in order to find out how well it satisfies GETout's initial design brief and the specification you developed.

As well as testing and evaluating your solution, you also need to comment on how well you have worked.

Testing the Final Solution

Go back to the design specification you wrote for your container or garment. Go through each statement and think about how you can check it. Some things may be very easy to test, while others might require you to set up a special test. For example you might:

▷ test it yourself – for example by putting all the relevant items in it and carrying it
▷ get an intended user to test it
▷ ask an expert such as someone at a local specialist shop or your teacher to try it out and give you their opinion.

If you can, take photographs of your product being used.

Remember to record the results of your tests. Write up the results and conclusions of all data collected.

Criteria	Method of testing	Extent to which it has been achieved
It must carry...	All items put into bag Older brother asked to put items into bag	My container holds all the items intended. A little bit of room for something extra.
Durability	Manager of local trek shop asked for opinion	The main part of the container should last well. The removable outside pocket is rather flimsy.

Evaluating your Designing and Making

In the light of the tests you have carried out, make an overall evaluation of the design you have come up with. You will also need to review the way your design has developed during the project. How successful was the making?

▷ What changes did you make and why?
▷ Did it turn out as intended?
▷ If not, why not?

Use diagrams to explain your answer.

You should also comment on how well you planned your work.

▷ Did you spend too long or not enough time on your investigation, designing, planning, making or evaluating?
▷ How closely were you able to keep to your time plan during the making process?

Improvements

Finish off by making positive suggestions for improvements to the design, and the way you worked.

List the things you could improve if you were to do it again.

Strengths	Areas for improvement
Stitching very neat	I could do more initial ideas as I tend to go straight for the final solution.
Pattern worked really well	I could have examined my research material more thoroughly.

Overall quality   Comment

Design – shape
   style
   ergonomics
   aesthetics

Making – seams
   finishing edges
   techniques
   top-stitching

Examination Questions

You should spend about one and a half hours answering the questions on this page or the next, as instructed by your teacher. You will need some paper, basic drawing equipment, and colouring materials. You are reminded of the need for good English and clear presentation in your answers.

Before you start the following questions you will need to do some preliminary research into:
● modern fabrics and fabric finishes used to make either high fashion club wear or decorative textiles products
● the use of a 'futuristic' theme in the design of such products

Design Brief

The designer for a small chain of fashion outlets is designing a range of clothing and decorative textiles products with a futuristic theme.

You should choose **either** fashion club wear **or** decorative textiles products. Answer the questions about the products you have chosen.

You have been asked you to advise on the choice of fabrics.

1. This question is about qualities needed in either fashion club wear or decorative textiles products. *(Total 18 marks).* See pages 56-59, 64-65

(a) (i) Describe the performance qualities needed in the fabrics in order to make them acceptable to the target market. *(8 marks)*
(ii) Explain how the qualities of fabrics used in the products can be used to reflect the futuristic theme. *(6marks)*
(b) A manufacturer will need to be sure that fabrics chosen for club wear have the qualities identified as being important. Explain how ICT can be used to help choose appropriate fabrics. *(4 marks)*

2. **This question is about the properties of modern fabrics.** *(Total 20 marks).* See pages 62-63, 64-65

(a) Many modern fabrics used for fashion and decorative products contain synthetic fibres. Explain why synthetic fibres are so popular for these garments. *(8 marks)*

(b) Fabrics are often given finishes to make them easier to care for or to give a special effect. Describe one of these finishes and explain why you might recommend its use on fabrics for your products. *(4 marks)*

(c) Explain how the construction method used for the fabric will affect the appearance and feel of fabrics used for your products. *(8 marks)*

3. **This question is about manufacture of the fashion club wear or decorative textiles products.** *(Total 29 marks).* See pages 68-69, 70-71

(a) The designer has chosen a stretchy fabric for one of the products.

(i) Give two problems that the use of this fabric may cause at each of the following stages of manufacture and suggest how they can be overcome:
● cutting out *(6 marks)*
● stitching of the seams *(6 marks)*
● using interfacings and linings *(6 marks)*

(ii) Describe two components that could be used in the product. Explain what will need to be considered when choosing them. *(6 marks)*

(b) A basic pattern which has been used successfully before is to be used for the product.

(i) Give two advantages of using a basic pattern. *(2 marks)*
(ii) Give three reasons why it would still be advisable to make a sample product before going ahead with mass manufacture. *(3 marks)*

4. **This question is about consumer issues related to fabrics.** *(Total 13 marks).* See pages 60, 72

(a) The product will have information labels attached to it.

(i) Give three things that might be included on a label. *(3 marks)*
(ii) How will legal requirements affect the information put on the product label? *(4 marks)*

(b) Many products for club wear have designer labels or logos. Discuss the advantages and disadvantages of buying products with designer labels. *(6 marks)*

Total marks = 80

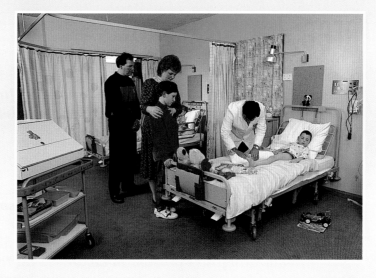

Before you start the following questions you will need to do some preliminary research into:

- modern fabrics in use for hospital furnishing and uniforms
- the use of colour and texture in the design of an environment or uniforms

Design Brief

A national health service trust wants to improve facilities in the children's wards in its group of hospitals. A range of furnishing items, including curtains, bedcovers and seating and uniforms for nursing staff is being designed for these areas.

You should choose **either** furnishing items **or** uniforms. Answer the questions about the products you have chosen.

You have been asked you to advise on the choice of fabrics.

1. **This question is about qualities needed in furnishings or uniforms for hospital environments.** *(Total 22 marks).* See pages 56-59, 64-67

(a) (i) Describe and give reasons for the performance qualities needed in the fabrics **either** bedcovers **or** trousers for nursing staff in order to make them acceptable for the specified end use. *(8 marks)*

(ii) Identify one quality which you consider to be important. Describe a test which could be carried out to check whether or not a fabric has this quality. Include details of:

- the equipment needed
- the method to be used
- how you would interpret the results *(8 marks)*

(b) How can texture and colour of furnishing and uniforms fabrics help to create a comfortable environment for the wards?

(6 marks)

2. **This question is about the properties of modern fabrics.** *(Total 14 marks).* See pages 56-57, 62-65

(a) Modern fabrics used for seating in public buildings **or** protective clothing for staff often contain synthetic fibres. Explain how the properties of these fibres make them appropriate for this use.

(8 marks)

(b) Explain how the construction of a fabric can help create an interesting colour or pattern in the fabric. *(6 marks)*

3. **This question is about manufacture of the furnishings or uniforms.** *(Total 44 marks).* See pages 68-71, 73

(a) The manufacturer will be working to a budget when making the products.

(i) Explain how computer technology can help keep costs down when planning the layout of the pattern on the fabric. *(4 marks)*

(ii) In what ways can costs be kept to a minimum when ordering fabrics and components for the products? *(3 marks)*

(b) Describe, with reasons, the manufacturing system you would recommend for the products.

(6 marks)

(c) The bedcovers and uniforms are to have the trust's logo on them for identification purposes.

(i) Evaluate the suitability of two different ways of putting a logo on these products. *(6 marks)*

(ii) Explain the benefits of using CAM in the manufacture of the logo. *(3 marks)*

(d) Describe and evaluate the suitability of two different seams which could be used when making **either** curtains to go round beds **or** trousers for nursing staff. *(6 marks)*

(e) Use notes and diagrams to explain how to make a hem at the bottom of either the curtains or the trousers. *(6 marks)*

(f) Quality control have identified the following problems. Explain the possible causes of each and explain how they can be put right:

(i) logos not in the same place on each product *(2 marks)*
(ii) a batch of bedcovers are not the same size *(4 marks)*
(iii) large holes made by machine needles *(2 marks)*
(iv) seams breaking *(2 marks)*

Total marks = 80

Project Three: Introduction

*Luxor Travel **need ideas for furnishing fabric designs and a uniform for the crew of their luxury cruise liner.***

***You have been asked to design and print a fabric based on an Egyptian** motif.*

This will be used to help co-ordinate visually the cabins and deck areas and the crew uniform. You will need to make up samples of your designs to present to** Luxor Travel **for consideration.

Quality Counts
(page 130)

Green Textiles
(page 134)

CAD-CAM
(pages 126 and 128)

Production
Process Systems
(pages 122 and 124)

The Brief

Luxor Travel would like to commission young designers to create the cabins and uniforms for their luxury ship which will cruise the Nile. They want the designs to reflect the wealth of history, richness of colour and opulence of ancient Egypt.

Furnishings

You are asked to design a fabric suitable for use in the cabin interior. The fabric design could be used for bedding, cushions, curtains, pelmets, etc., or as decorative hangings. You will need to:

▷ design and make a length of fabric
▷ make up one or more of the items above from the fabric you make
▷ produce scale drawings and/or a presentation model of a cabin, indicating the overall colour scheme and where your fabric designs will be used.

Uniforms

Alternatively you could design a fabric and textile logo to be used for a range of uniforms for the cabin crew, e.g. T-shirts, waistcoats, headscarves, etc. You will need to print the fabric and make up one or more of these items.

Manufacturing the fabrics

The fabric and textile products you design would need to be produced in quantity. *Luxor Travel* would need to know how you plan to make the amount they need quickly and to a consistently high standard.

The company is particularly concerned that the fabrics, dyes and construction methods they use will cause the minimum amount of damage to the environment.

They would therefore like you to prepare a short report advising them on how the products will be manufactured in quantity.

The
Gift
of The
Nile

ADVERTISEMENT

The Gift of The Nile

Herodotus, a 5th Century B.C. Greek historian, called Egypt the 'Gift of the Nile'. The 'Gift of the Nile' will commence its Nile Cruise at the Valley of the Kings at Thebes, Luxor, travelling up to Cairo and then onto Alexandra.

Its passengers will experience the breath-taking architecture of the pyramids and the sphinx, see riches from the burial chambers of Pharoahs like Tutankhamen and decipher the stories hidden in the Hieroglyphics.

MAIDEN VOYAGE

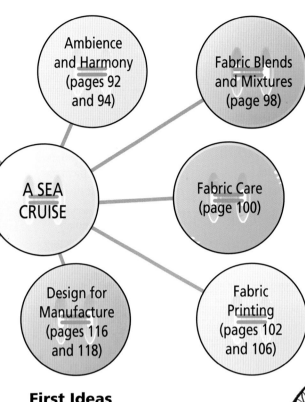

First Ideas

From your research, pick out a range of shapes, colours and patterns that you feel are typical of ancient Egypt. Begin to manipulate these images by:

▷ changing the sizes of shapes in relation to one another
▷ by repeating a chosen image
▷ by rotating a shape or image
▷ by interchanging the colours
▷ by cutting up a photocopy of a design and rearranging the pieces.

You could use a computer to generate these ideas.

Investigation

Using the library and travel brochures for Egypt from travel agents, research the theme of ancient Egypt. Find out more about its history, e.g.:

▷ Tutankhamun
▷ Howard Carter
▷ hieroglyphics.

In particular look out for examples of the patterns, textures and colours of the clothes and jewellery worn by rich Egyptian men and women.

What did a typical Egyptian interior look like? Sketch architectural details, patterns and colours. A lot of decorative detail can be found on ceramics and in the hieroglyphics.

Put together swatches of fabrics with different textures, patterns and colour tones which are based on your research. Think about how well they combine together or use complementary colours to provide a more vivid contrast.

You could use a CAD program to help do this.

A SEA CRUISE

starting point

Inside Out (1): the Cabin and the Cushion

Colours, textures, patterns and lighting effects all combine together to make interior spaces and places comfortable to be in. The size and shape of the space and how the objects within it, such as soft-furnishings, are arranged, together with the materials used, determine its practicality.

 ICT

Designers use CAD to develop designs that can show how a room layout may look. Decisions can be made quickly about the scale of design as well as colours, and through texture mapping what type of fabric structure might be used - i.e. woven or knitted.

Designing interior spaces

The interior spaces I design are intended to create a comfortable working environment with a distinctive feel. A feature chosen from a particular period in history or from an individual culture can inspire the rest of the space. Colourways, patterns and textures can then be developed through exploring the chosen theme further. Lighting can often be used creatively to enhance the overall effect.

I start by looking at the function of the space and begin to plan around its purpose. For example, a kitchen needs facilities for food storage, preparation, cooking, serving and for washing up. I decide where best to place these areas in relation to each other so that the user can work effectively and safely.

Circulation, or how we move through a space, is very important, especially if there is more than one person in the room.

Next I would look at the most suitable materials for the kitchen furniture, floor and wall coverings, and the soft furnishings. Considerations of scratch, soil and heat resistance, as well as serviceability for fabrics (washing) are very important.

The shape and size of a room, as well as the amount of natural light it receives, will influence the choice of colours, patterns and textures. A small room, with limited natural light, would favour light colours, smaller patterns, reflective surfaces and the clever use of artificial light to exaggerate the feeling of height and spaciousness. Conversely, in a large, well illuminated space, darker and bolder patterned fabrics could give a more intimate or cosy feel to the room.

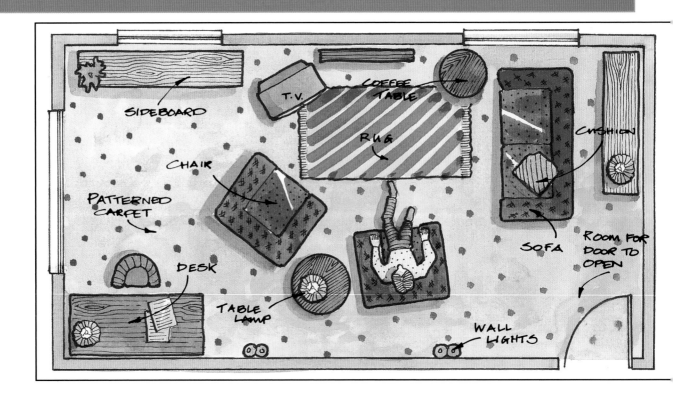

SIDEBOARD

T.V.

COFFEE TABLE

CUSHION

CHAIR

RUG

PATTERNED CARPET

DESK

SOFA

ROOM FOR DOOR TO OPEN

TABLE LAMP

WALL LIGHTS

Soft Furnishings Product Analysis

You will need to make a study of how **soft furnishings** are designed, constructed and finished.

Looking at existing products in detail and taking them apart to discover how they have been assembled is a good way to do this. Alternatively, just look at the product and turn it inside out to see how it is constructed.

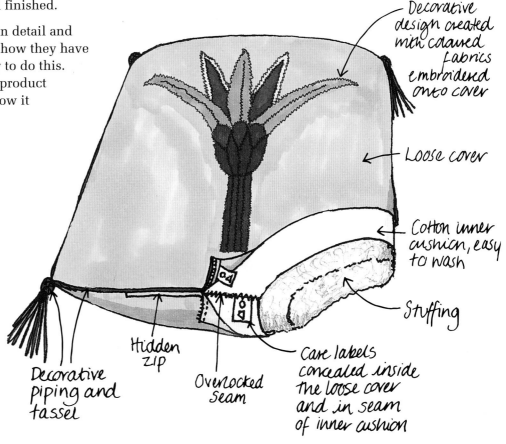

Decorative design created with coloured fabrics embroidered onto cover

Loose cover

Cotton inner cushion, easy to wash

Stuffing

Care labels concealed inside the loose cover and in seam of inner cushion

Decorative piping and tassel

Hidden ZIP

Overlocked Seam

■ ACTIVITY

You will need to find a cushion cover or bolster. Make sketches of the different designs, shapes, fastenings, enhancements and finishes. Describe your findings.

■ ACTIVITY

Choose a room at home or school. Describe and comment on the following :

► the intended use of the room – does it suit its purpose?
► the appropriateness of furniture and fittings.
► the circulation through the space – is there room to move easily and safely?
► the use of artificial light, e.g. table lamps, uplighters.
► the focal point of the room, e.g. TV, fire place, etc.
► the use of soft and hard surfaces, e.g. carpet, parquet flooring, patterned and plain fabrics, different textures and mixtures of colour and reflective and matt surfaces.
► the use of decorative textiles, e.g. pelmets and cushions.
► how noisy the room is without the TV or radio on.

Does the room suit its function? How could it be improved?

■ ACTIVITY

Carry out a product analysis of a range of soft furnishing products used in different environments. Make sketches of the different designs, shapes, fastenings, enhancements and finishes. Record the effects of line, pattern, colour and texture.

► How have past styles influenced present trends?
► What sort of image and lifestyle do you think the products were designed for?

 WWW.

To find out more about the use of ICT in the design of room layouts go to:
www.nedgraphics.com
www.apso.com

KEY POINTS

● Colour and light can help create a mood in an environment.
● The shape and size of a room influences the choice of colours, patterns and textures used for furnishings.

Inside Out (2): Uniform Analysis

Uniforms serve many purposes. As well as being practical they say something about the people wearing them, and the company or organisation they belong to.

The shapes, colours, pattern and textures used all deliver messages about the quality and nature of the service being provided.

What effect are the people in the photographs creating by wearing their uniforms?

A **uniform** is an easily identifiable set of practical clothes which is unique to the role of the wearer. Uniforms help protect the wearer, ensure a basic standard of appearance, and often indicate seniority.

What we wear is a form of communication, whether we are wearing a uniform or casual clothes of our own choice.

You need to find out as much as possible about the purpose and design of uniforms to be able to define the needs of the company and of the people who will be wearing them.

■ ACTIVITY

1. In groups discuss the different reasons for wearing a uniform.

▷ Are uniforms really necessary?
▷ Do we lose our individuality by wearing a uniform?
▷ Are school uniforms a good idea?

2. Collect pictures from old magazines and make a collage of each of the following:

▷ special outfits worn to show authority.
▷ special uniforms for carrying out particular jobs.

Analyse the material collected. What items does a uniform usually include? What are the specific requirements for outfits worn by people working in the leisure and travel industries?

3. Carry out an investigation into uniforms. Do you know anyone who wears a uniform for work? Devise a survey to find out the advantages and disadvantages of their uniform.

Ergonomics

A uniform must be safe, comfortable and convenient. The individual wearing it must be able to carry out the work required with no restrictions. For example a soldier must be able to move well in his or her uniform.

Ease of maintenance, i.e. cleaning, pressing and repair, is also particulary important.

Garment Analysis and Evaluation

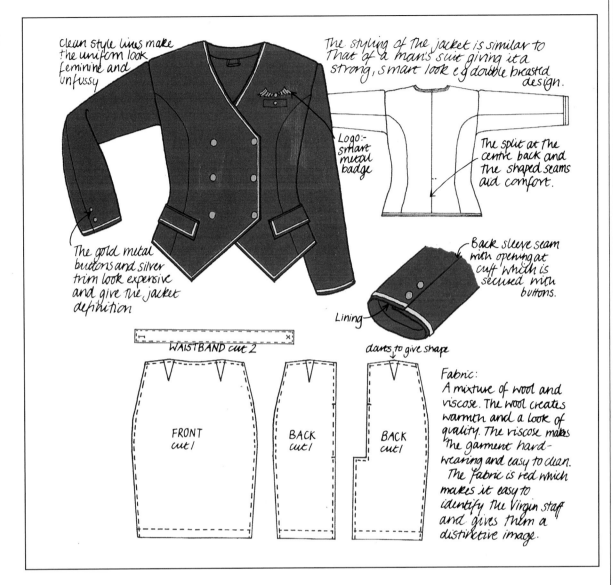

Clean style lines make the uniform look feminine and unfussy

The styling of the jacket is similar to that of a man's suit giving it a strong, smart look e.g double breasted design.

Logo:- smart metal badge

The split at the centre back and the shaped seams aid comfort.

The gold metal buttons and silver trim look expensive and give the jacket definition

Back sleeve seam with opening at cuff which is secured with buttons.

Lining

WAISTBAND cut 2

FRONT cut 1

BACK cut 1

BACK cut 1

darts to give shape

Fabric:
A mixture of wool and viscose. The wool creates warmth and a look of quality. The viscose makes the garment hard-wearing and easy to clean. The fabric is red which makes it easy to identify the Virgin staff and gives them a distinctive image.

■ ACTIVITY

Obtain a uniform to study, or work from the photographs on these pages.
- ▶ Where are the seams, topstitching, openings, etc?
- ▶ Describe the fibres and fabrics used. How might they have been printed or dyed?
- ▶ Have any trimmings or fastenings been used?

Try to draw the pattern pieces needed to make each garment.
- ▶ How has colour been used for these uniforms? Is it effective?
- ▶ Describe the logos and where they are placed. How distinctive are they?
- ▶ Is the uniform ergonomically sound?
- ▶ What do you think of the style of these uniforms?
- ▶ Do you think they are suitable for the working environment for which they were made?
- ▶ Can you suggest any improvements to the overall design?

KEY POINTS
- Uniforms convey information about the person wearing them and the company or organisation they belong to.
- They also need to be comfortable and practical.

Ambience and Harmony (1): Interior Spaces

A SEA CRUISE

Ambience *is the total effect achieved by everything on the ship, including the furnishings and fittings and uniforms. Harmony is achieved when all the different parts adapt well to each other to create a relaxed and comfortable ambience.*

By careful planning and designing it is possible to create the appropriate ambience for the intended users.

Ambience

Ambience describes a feeling we get about how well the things which exist in a particular space harmonise together.

When we walk into a room or space it should feel inviting and comfortable to use. One room may be very visually stimulating whereas another may be soothing, but they must both be welcoming.

Different things put together create a good ambience:

▷ lighting
▷ colour schemes
▷ patterns and textures
▷ hard and soft surfaces to sit on and walk on
▷ background noise reduced through carpets instead of hard flooring.

Line

Line also has an important part to play in the way we feel. Vertical lines are strong and stable, horizontal lines calming and diagonal lines dynamic. The use of line in your interior design, be it strong architectural features or in the surface pattern of a chosen fabric, can also give off emotional signals to the person using the space. Vertical lines can also make a room seem taller whilst horizontal lines will make it feel shorter and wider.

Lighting

Light in an interior space can create a lot of desirable and dramatic effects, and can be used to highlight features with spot lights or bathe a wall in soft light.

The different colours emitted by electric light bulbs alter the colours of the room illuminated.

Lighting is discussed on pages 32 to 33 and must be considered if a lot of artificial light is to appear in the interior space. Remember the room will be used in natural daylight as well as artificial light in the evening.

Colour

Can you remember what the following words mean: tint, hue, shade, contrasting, harmonious, primary and secondary colours? Discuss in a small group and write down your answers. The colour wheel and words used to describe the different uses of colour are explained on pages 36 to 39.

Colour associations

It is important to have an understanding of colour and the psychology or feelings associated with certain colours. For example red, seen in nature as fire, is associated with danger; blue the colour of the sea and sky, is associated with calm; white, the colour of clouds and snow, is associated with purity. What other colours can you think of and what associations do you make with them?

Colours can be described as warm (red and orange), or cool (blue and green), and can strongly influence an overall effect in an interior space. A room interior which is mainly tints and shades of blue would be very soothing, restful and cool. You must consider the effect of colour choices and work towards a desired feel. Try different combinations of colour and describe how you feel when looking at the colour combinations.

Colour plays a vital role in helping the designer achieve the right ambience. Remember that colour can affect our moods. Too much black, grey and neutral colour can make us feel down whereas brighter colours such as yellow may lift our spirits. At the same time too many contrasting bright colours will not help customers to relax.

IN YOUR PROJECT

▶ Experiment with the different light sources on different coloured fabrics and record your findings. Discuss your results in class.

▶ Think about the effect your colour choices will have on your interior space.

▶ It may be useful to get a colour chart from a DIY store and cut and paste your chosen colours together.

Colour harmony

Too many colours together can look hectic and unco-ordinated, whereas too few can look co-ordinated but dull. Colour schemes must try to be balanced, harmonious and pleasing.

Choose blends of colour that contrast light and dark tones. The palest colours should be used for large surfaces, the richer colours for decorative detailing.

There are three types of harmony:

▶ Monochrome harmony – tints and shades of the same hues.

▶ Related harmony – made up of small families of hues next to each other on the colour wheel. In order to exercise colour contrast, gradual steps in tone and colour intensity are used to create a visually pleasing effect.

▶ Contrast harmony – made up of contrasting hues opposite each other on the colour wheel.

Colour and proportion

In a room, interior colour can create many tricks of the eye. The cool hues of blues and greens make walls recede, and warm hues of red and yellow make the walls advance. A dark carpet, mid-toned walls and a light ceiling will add the feeling of height to a room. In a room with a dark carpet and ceiling, light walls will look wider and lower.

KEY POINTS

● Colour schemes need to be balanced, harmonious and pleasing to the eye.

● Colour is important in achieving the right ambience.

● Lines can be used to create optical illusions.

Ambience and Harmony (2): Creating Uniformity

A SEA CRUISE

Corporate Identity

All organisations, whether a school or a sea cruise travel company have an identity, although they may not necessarily be aware of it. **Corporate identity** is when the way the company is perceived by the public is deliberately engineered. What a company does and how it does it can all be expressed through the following areas.

Environments

This is the atmosphere created on the boat. This is crucial in putting across the right message to the customer. Visual identity can have the most significant impact so the designer responsible for uniforms, logos and interiors etc. has a vital role to play.

Products and services

This includes the holidays offered by the company and all the services available while on board the ship including entertainment, food served etc.

Communications

This is how you explain what your company does through advertising and any other printed material. Staff are important too as how they communicate with the customer will have an influence on them.

It is essential that all the different elements of a corporate identity system work together in harmony.

Colour and Self-image

We like to wear colours we feel comfortable in and that suit our complexion and colouring. They may also reflect our general outlook on life. For example vivid colours can be worn to reflect an outgoing personality or mood, while paler colours can reflect a quieter personality or mood.

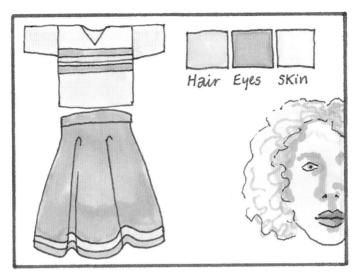

■ ACTIVITY

▶ Draw a quick self-portrait. Shade in the colour of your eyes, hair and skin.
▶ Sketch an outfit to harmonise with your colouring.
▶ Sketch another using contrasting colours which would be suitable for going out with friends.

Remember the shape of the garments can create an effect as well.

Creating the Right Impression

It is helpful to understand more about the impression the colour of our clothes creates.

▷ Dark blues, blacks and greys suggest respect and authority.
▷ Fawn coloured clothes, especially when combined with soft blue, look professional but are less threatening, so encourage a more open conversation.
▷ Brown clothes suggest a lack of authority.
▷ Green clothes can give an 'off-duty', recreational impression.

Which of these colours of clothes would you wear for presenting your work to a client, interviewing someone or going out for the evening?

IN YOUR PROJECT

▶ What sort of image do you think the various staff members should project through their uniforms.
▶ How can colour help achieve this image?

KEY POINTS

● Corporate identity is important in promoting a company and its services.
● It can be expressed through the way in which its environments, products and services and communications work together in harmony.
● The colours people wear create an impression on others.

In the Mood

A SEA CRUISE

You will need to do some further research into what people expect and want on a cruise. Creating a moodboard will help you find a range of colours, textures and patterns that work well together and appeal to passengers.

Many textile companies use ICT to help create Moodboards. They also use them to create Trend Boards, which they use to help them define the market that their products are aimed at and show what they might be designing in the future. To find out more, go to: **www.etexx.com**

Further Investigation

Your research needs to be relevant and can be found in many obvious places: the library, magazines, from talking to experts, etc. **Primary research** involves conducting interviews or experiments to gain new information. **Secondary research** is using information found out by someone else. Your results need to be recorded and presented in an effective way.

Literature search

You will need to collect and collate as much secondary research material as possible in the time allowed. Library books are a good source of text, descriptions and pictures, especially museum catalogues on Egyptian exhibitions (e.g. The British Museum). Brochures from holiday companies provide material that can be cut out. What other sources or research can you think of?

Questionnaire

A questionnaire provides a primary source of information which you can then interpret and apply to your project. You are asked to design a cabin for a luxury cruise liner, so you need to find out what expectations potential customers would have, what facilities they would expect to have in their luxury cabins and what types of finishes to the room they would find pleasing.

Remember to add further questions of your own to the ones shown. Check that the questions will provide helpful information. Present your results in the form of a table.

Moodboards

A **moodboard** is an excellent way to assemble a range of visual research material as a source of inspiration for ideas. The visual material may include fabric swatches, textured and coloured papers, historical design sources, photographs and computer images. You could also include key words to stimulate your ideas further. Together they should create the feel or ambience of your intended interior, fabrics or uniforms. A moodboard will also help you to see how well different elements, such as curtain fabrics and particular paint colours work together.

As you create your moodboard, imagine how you want people to feel when they walk into your interior or see someone wearing a uniform. You may want to prepare a different moodboard for different areas of the cruise liner, or for different uniforms.

The moodboard should then inform your designing. When it is completed keep it where it can be seen when you are developing your ideas.

Questionnaire

What age group are you in: 15-25, 26-35, 36-45, 46 and above?

Have you ever been to Egypt?

What images do you associate with Egypt, e.g. pyramids, hieroglyphics etc?

Which colours would you associate with Egypt?

Have you ever been on a cruise?

What would you expect to find in a cabin on a cruise liner?

Create your own moodboard.
Ask your teacher and fellow students to describe what they feel when they look at your moodboard. Try to get them to use helpful descriptive words like luxurious, warm, cosy, welcoming, cold, clinical, etc.

▷ Is your moodboard successful?

▷ How could you make it better?

You could use your moodboard as part of your research to find out what potential customers think.

Shapes and sizes

The resources for your moodboard should be cut into similar shapes such as geometric (squares, triangles, circles etc.) or organic (asymmetrical or random) shapes of different sizes, or a combination of both.

Don't go for the easy option of just using the shapes your resources come in, but cut them to suit what you want. Think about the size of the base board you will be using. A3 or A2 is a good size, but it could be larger or smaller.

KEY POINTS

- Detailed research helps designers decide what will sell well.
- Mood boards can be useful in putting ideas together and promoting images.

ICT ➡

You could use ICT to help you in developing a layout for your board; you can scan in images and manipulate them using a graphics program.

Layout

Before you finally stick your samples down, try several alternative ways of presenting them.

Experiment by mixing different shapes, sizes and contrasts of sheen and matt fabrics, etc. Aim to achieve a good balance of colour and space across the board. Make sure the central area contains the strongest visual focus.

Very vibrant and rich samples should appear in small amounts if mixed with lighter tones of fabric, otherwise they will overwhelm the desired effect of the final presentation.

Pattern Repeats

Patterns are developed by repeating one or more shapes and colours. There are a variety of methods which can be used to work out a pattern repeat.

To find out more about using ICT to create automatic repeats go to:
www.nedgraphics.com
www.lectra.com
www.speedstep.de

Mirror Repeat

A mirror image reflects a pattern as it might be viewed in a mirror. Fold your paper in half and produce a design on one half of the paper. This image can be turned over and held up to a light-box or window, and then traced.

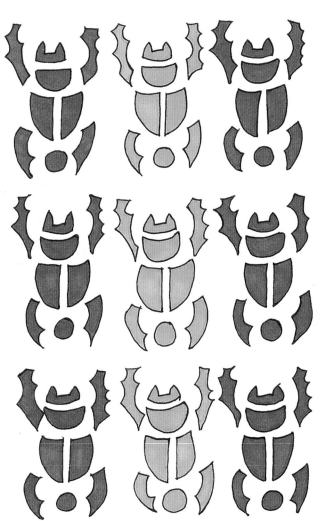

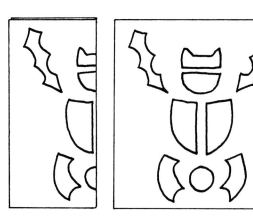

Straight Repeat

A straight repeat can be produced by repeating your motif at measured intervals, placing each motif directly under the previous one.

Half-drop Repeat

A half-drop repeat is produced by repeating the motif at the side as before, but moving the design half a measurement along underneath, like a brick pattern.

Joined Straight Repeat

A joined straight repeat is produced by:

▷ deciding on the size of your repeat
▷ cutting the paper to size
▷ drawing the motif in the centre of the paper
▷ cutting the sides to join up the pattern
▷ cutting the top and bottom to join up the pattern

Joined up Half-drop

This is achieved by:

▷ deciding on the size of your repeat
▷ cutting the paper to size
▷ drawing the motif in the centre of the paper
▷ dividing the paper to exact quarters
▷ cutting the sides to join up the pattern
▷ joining up the top right quarter with the bottom left quarter to continue to repeat the pattern
▷ joining up the top left quarter with the bottom right quarter to continue to repeat the pattern.

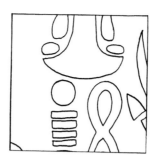

ICT ➡

Digital printing uses special dyes and inks. These need to be fixed to the fabric after printing by steaming. The main advantages of digital printing are:

- designs can be produced in hours – from concept to end-product
- clients can make decisions about colourways and fabric types instantly
- sample prototypes and fabrics can all be printed in the same way

IN YOUR PROJECT

▶ Experiment with the different shapes and colours of your theme to see if you can develop a successful design.
▶ Try out a variety of methods of working out a pattern repeat.

A SEA CRUISE

enhancement of fabrics

Fabric Blends and Mixtures

Choosing the right fibre and fabric is not always simple. A fibre is rarely perfect and able to give us all the properties we want. Today many fabrics are used which are composed of fibre blends or mixtures.

Blends

This is when two or more different fibres are used to produce a yarn. The fibres are blended before or during spinning. Polyester/cotton is one that is commonly used.

Mixtures

This is when a fabric is made of two or more different fibres, each one spun into a separate yarn. A fabric could have a cotton warp and a woollen weft and it would be described as a wool and cotton mix.

Why have mixtures and blends?

1. To unite the different properties of two or more fibres in order to cover up less desirable characteristics in any of the fibres and give an improved fabric performance.

For example polyester is not very absorbent, dries quickly, does not crease and is easy to iron. Cotton is highly absorbent, takes a long time to dry, creases a lot and is difficult to iron. A blend of both fibres will balance out the properties giving an easy-care fabric whilst retaining the more desirable qualities of cotton such as softness and warmth.

2. To reduce costs by blending or mixing a cheap fibre with a more expensive one.

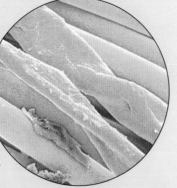

3. To give different texture and colour effects by using filament and staple yarns which have different textures and dye differently. All fibres do not take up dye easily because some are more absorbent than others. This means that when different fibres are spun together and dyed an interesting effect is produced as the fibres are not all the same colour. This is known as cross-dyeing.

Safety

The ease with which a textile product burns depends on many things including the fibre or blends of fibre used. The chart shows the level of **flammability** of some common fibres.

High Flammability	Low Flammability
Cotton	Cotton treated with flame retardants
Linen	
Acetate	Flame resistant acetate
Rayon	Flame retardent rayon
Acrylic	Polyester
Blends and mixes containing a lot of fibres of low flammability	

Why should polyester cotton be so flammable when polyester is a fibre of low flammability?

Polyester fibres are thermoplastic and normally extinguish themselves by the falling away of the burning molten material. If cotton is present as well it supports the molten polyester and prevents it from dropping and consequently the fabric burns fiercely.

If a cotton sewing thread is used in a polyester fabric the flame will run along the length of the stitching. This is why the Nightdress (Safety) Regulations 1967 insist that thermoplastic sewing threads must be used below the waist or elbow in nightdresses made from a thermoplastic material.

Combining Fabrics

A wide range of the fabrics are now available. Different fabrics can be effectively combined together. The balance between waterproofness, breathability, fabric handling and appearance can be chosen to suit a particular application. For example:

▷ interfacing can be combined with fabric to produce strength and stiffness

▷ quilting different fabrics in layers can provide added warmth.

There are two methods of combining fabrics:

▷ Coating – a layer or layers of a polymer film is applied to the surface of a base fabric.

▷ Laminating – this is when two or more layers of fabric are combined by an intermediate layer of polymer which adheres to both surfaces.

Coated and laminated fabrics are made in many weights and constructions for a variety of applications.

Coated fabrics are frequently chosen for their ability to keep the wearer dry in a storm, while still allowing perspiration from the body to escape. These are often known as 'breathable fabrics'. They conduct the perspiration to the outer surface along a chain of hydrophilic (water attractive) molecules.

Coated fabrics are also used to make protective garments needed in agriculture and industry. PVC coatings applied to cotton or viscose give protection against acid and alkali splashes.

Laminated fabrics allow the attractive appearance of an unstable knitted or lace fabric to be combined with the stability of a woven fabric and provide a much firmer handle.

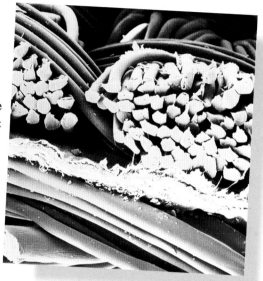

Gore-Tex waterproof fabric (x100). This resembles a sandwich with nylon outer layers and porous teflon filling

A SEA CRUISE

enhancement of fabrics

■ ACTIVITY

1. Carry out an investigation into the blends and mixtures most commonly used for clothing and soft furnishings. Use the fibre property chart on page 65 to work out why the particular fibres have been combined. Record your results and conclusions in your fabric swatch book.

In your project folder write down the properties that you think are the most important for the following textile items on board the cruise liner:
▶ uniforms for various crew members
▶ bed linen
▶ soft furnishings.

2. In groups discuss the particular safety factors which would need to be considered for textile products used on board a ship.

3. Carry out an investigation into reversible fabrics. How many examples can you find in everyday use? Record your results in your fabric swatch book.

Uses of laminated and coated fabrics

Leisure-wear:
tents and sleeping bag covers
anoraks
cagoules
overtrainers
gloves
ski-wear
sportswear\footwear

Work:
specialised tarpaulins
survival suits
foul weather clothing
military clothing
surgical clothing (disposables)
hospital drapes
mattress and seat covers

Rainproof fabric (x30). The outer surface is covered with a polyurethane layer which has tiny pores. This coating is known as 'breathable waterproofing'

KEY POINTS

● Fibres and yarns are often mixed or blended to produce particular properties in a fabric.
● Polyester/cotton is one of the most common blends.
● Some blends and mixtures can result in a fabric that is highly flammable.

Fabric Care

Because modern textile items are made from a wide range of fibres and fabrics, they need to be laundered in different ways.

Public laundry, Kensal Green, London, 1883

A modern industrial laundry

Standardising Fabric Care

An **International Textile Care Labelling Code (ITCLC)** which everyone can understand has been developed. This makes it easier to choose the correct cleaning method for each garment.

Manufacturers of washing machines also use this code to standardise their washing programs. The care code appears on labels, detergent packets and washing machines.

In the UK instructions on the use and care of textile products are voluntary, but when a product does carry a label it becomes a legal requirement that the recommendations on the label are appropriate. Such a label should be permanently fixed to the article.

Care Labelling

It is of great benefit to consumers that all garments carry a care label which must state the fibre content of a garment. A good label will contain the following information:

▷ fibre content (this is compulsory)
▷ any special treatments or finishes
▷ cleaning instructions
▷ size of garment.

These labels are permanently stitched into the garment.

Informative Labelling

These labels carry extra information and are only temporarily attached to the garment.

Some good examples of these labels are shown on the right.

PURE NEW WOOL

The Woolmark was launched internationally by the International Wool Secretariat in 1964. This label may only be used by approved manufacturers whose fabrics have met the quality and performance standards laid down by the IWS. The IWS regularly checks this merchandise to ensure that the textile contains the right fibre content and maintains the appropriate required standard with respect to characteristics such as shrink resistance, tensile strength, colour fastness and moth proofing.

Textile Care Code

Washing

Symbol	Meaning
⊔40°	Maximum temperature 40°C Mechanical action normal Rinsing and spinning normal
⊔40°	Maximum temperature 40°C Mechanical action reduced Rinse with gradual cooling Spinning reduced
⊔40°	Maximum temperature 40° Mechanical action much reduced Rinsing/spinning normal
⊔ (hand)	Hand wash only

Washing continued

Symbol	Meaning
⊠	Do not wash
△CL	Chlorine bleach can be used
⊠	Do not bleach

Ironing

Symbol	Meaning
iron (one dot)	Cool iron
iron (two dots)	Warm iron
iron (three dots)	Hot iron
iron crossed	Do not iron

Drying

Symbol	Meaning
○ in square	Tumble drying beneficial
⊠ in square	Do not tumble dry
|||	Drip dry, soaking wet
—	Dry flat
⌣	Hang to dry

Dry cleaning

Symbol	Meaning
Ⓐ	Dry clean in all solvents
Ⓟ	Dry clean in perchloroethylene
Ⓕ	Dry clean in certain solvents only
⊗	Do not dry clean

■ ACTIVITIES

1. On the right is a label from a dress.

Explain how the dress should be cleaned.

2. Using the textile care symbols, design a label for a shirt which should be washed at no more than 50°C on a normal cycle, ironed with a warm iron and which must be hung to be dried.

3. Make your own chart of textile care labels in your fabric swatch book. Use the textile care labels to explain what the instructions mean. Look at soft furnishings as well as garments.

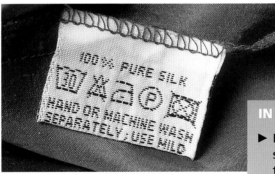

Item	Fibre content	Label symbols	Meaning
Jumper	100% cotton	⊔50°	Maxi temp – 50o
		Ⓟ	Reduced mechanical action
		⊠	Do not bleach
		iron (two dots)	Warm Iron
		○ in square	Tumble Dry

KEY POINTS

● Fabric care has been standardised by the use of a Care Labelling Code.

● Care labels are permanent and informative labels are temporary.

● Fabric care is related to the properties of the fibre(s) and fabric construction.

IN YOUR PROJECT

▶ Brainstorm any special requirements to be taken into consideration when laundering uniforms, bedding (sheets and pillowcases) and soft furnishings.

▶ Investigate whether it would be more expensive to dry clean uniforms or have someone launder them on the premises. What are the implications of being on board a sea cruise liner?

Fabric Printing (1)

A SEA CRUISE

There are three basic methods of printing onto fabric:

▷ *block printing*
▷ *roller printing*
▷ *rotary and flat-bed screen printing.*

The one you choose will depend on the quantity and quality you require and what the fabric will eventually be used for.

You also need to work out the appropriate size and repeat pattern for the fabric.

Block Printing

This craft is over 2000 years old. Traditionally, it is done using wooden or metal blocks. Until 1785, all fabric printing was done by hand blocking. This proved to be an expensive method of producing large quantities of decorated fabrics.

The design is prepared on the block by cutting away the background so that the design area is raised. The dye is applied to the raised surface of the block and the block is then placed onto the fabric. The disadvantages of this process are:

▷ it is very time consuming
▷ it requires a different block for each colour
▷ it is unsatisfactory if fine detail is required.

1 Draw a simple shape onto the surface of your block.

2 Carefully cut away the background so that the design is raised.

3 Press the block into some ink on the plate.

4 Press the inked block onto the paper or fabric.

■ ACTIVITY

You will require:
▶ a printing block made from lino, potato or a block of balsa wood
▶ a sharp craft knife
▶ printing ink
▶ a plate and brush
▶ scrap newspaper
▶ paper or fabric to print on.

Repeat and evaluate the technique. Does it give consistent results?

You might like to try a block where the shape is cut away and the background is raised.

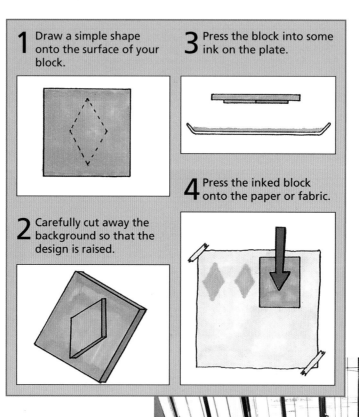

Block printing in Bangladesh

Roller Printing

Roller printing was invented by a Scotsman called Bell. This method speeded up the production of printed fabrics and allowed the simultaneous application of several different coloured dyes in the process.

The process is cheap to run, but has a number of disadvantages:

▷ the rollers are very expensive
▷ the size of the pattern is limited to the circumference of the roller, usually a maximum of 50 cm
▷ it can be difficult to print large patches of colour without blotches.

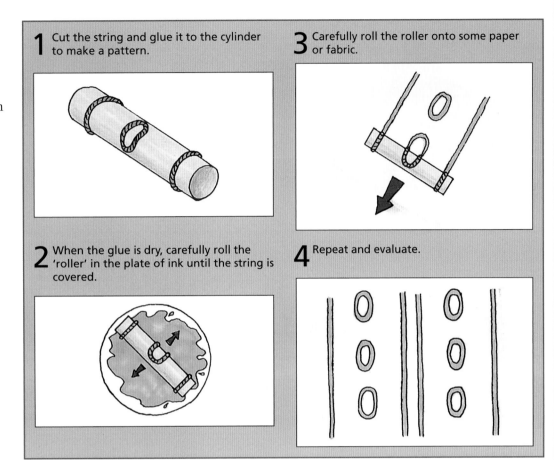

1 Cut the string and glue it to the cylinder to make a pattern.

2 When the glue is dry, carefully roll the 'roller' in the plate of ink until the string is covered.

3 Carefully roll the roller onto some paper or fabric.

4 Repeat and evaluate.

Rotary Screen Printing

Rotary screen printing is the fastest and most widely used process. Modern machines can print over 300 m of fabric per minute. A different colour is pumped into each cylinder and is forced out through a fine mesh screen onto the fabric passing below. The circumference of the roller determines the size of the design repeat.

■ ACTIVITY

Another method used for industrial printing is called 'heat transfer'. The design is printed in special ink on paper and then transferred to the cloth using heat and pressure. Ask if you can do a simplified version of this in school.

Roller printing a fabric

■ ACTIVITY

You will need;
▶ a small cylinder e.g. a piece of dowel, a toilet roll
▶ printing ink
▶ a large plate and a brush
▶ some string and glue
▶ scrap newspaper
▶ paper or fabric to print on.

KEY POINTS

In industry there are four main printing machine processes:
● roller printing
● rotary screen printing
● flat-bed screen printing
● heat transfer

Fabric Printing (2)

A SEA CRUISE

Flat-bed Screen Printing

Screen printing was developed from the stencil printing used a lot in Japan. To stop the middles falling out of stencil designs, little tabs had to be left behind. However in screen printing, the design is placed beneath the fine mesh of the screen, so intricate patterns can be achieved without worrying about the design collapsing.

Screens are economical to print with and complicated designs with fine detail can be printed well. They are also good for printing large areas of colour.

In industrial flat-bed screen printing, the squeegee is replaced by metal rods which are propelled backwards and forwards by magnets below the screen. Many screens can be used in sequence to produce complicated and colourful designs.

■ ACTIVITY

You will need;
- a simple A4 wooden frame
- some organdie
- a stapler
- masking tape
- a squeegee
- printing ink
- scrap newspaper
- paper or fabric to print on.

The process of making a screen is covered in Stages 1 and 2. You may not need to do this.

1 Staple the organdie onto the frame as tightly as possible.

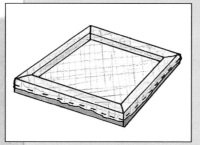

2 Stick the masking tape around the underside of the screen where the organdie touches the wooden frame. This will stop the ink leaking out.

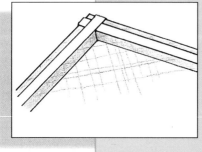

3 Make your stencil out of paper, cutting out a simple design.

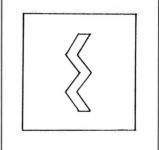

4 Place the stencil underneath the frame, but on top of a piece of plain paper.

5 Pour a thick line of ink at one end of the screen.

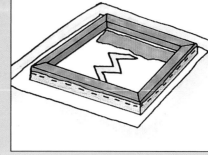

6 Using the squeegee, press down and draw the ink across the screen. Ask someone else to hold the screen to stop it moving.

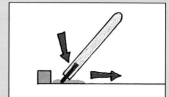

7 Carefully lift the screen off.

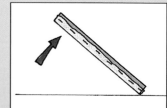

8 Repeat and evaluate.

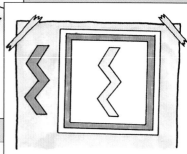

Industrial Case Study

Andrew Martin International

Andrew Martin International produce fabrics for furniture.

1 The process begins with one of their freelance textile designers developing a fabric which will be suitable to print, and then be fixed and finished.

2 Bleached fabric is used for printing to make sure the colours reproduce correctly. The design is printed through a series of screens. This gradually builds up the pattern, colour by colour.

3 A magnetic roller applies dye evenly over the whole screen, but the dye only passes through the screen where the dye is to appear. This is known as continuous flat bed screen printing. The way the fabric is printed affects the final look.

4 The dyes used are not colourfast, so they must be fixed into the fabric. To achieve this, the fabric is passed through a fixer. This changes its colour however.

5 To restore the original colour, the fabric is given a bath in acetic acid. This acid is then washed out, and the fabric dried again.

6 The cloth is tinted to give it its yellow antique effect. It is then stretched in a drier to restore the original dimensions after its many washes.

7 Finally it is checked for colour consistency, weave and pattern faults before the pattern cutter can get to work. Because the pattern has a strong motif, it's critical that the cutter takes the design into account while he's marking up and cutting.

A SEA CRUISE

enhancement of fabrics

Specification/Developing Ideas: the Cabin

You will need to develop a specification and designs for a co-ordinated range of two and three-dimensional textile products for the cabin, based on an Egyptian theme.

You will then need to decide which to print and make up into a sample to show to Luxor Travel.

► What different types of floor covering could be used for wet and dry areas?.
► Where could you gain extra storage?
► Where could you use artificial light sources?
► Where could you drape fabric to add interest and drama?
► How could you make the cabin look bigger?

Specification

The **design specification** is the set of targets you need to meet. Before you can begin your final design you need a more detailed list of requirements for the facilities, furniture and function for your cabin.

It may be helpful to look at photographs of existing cabins from holiday cruise brochures and makes notes of the list of facilities available. Assume that one to two people will be using each cabin.

▷ How many different areas would the cabin be split into e.g. for sleeping, bathing etc.?
▷ What facilities would passengers expect to find in their cabin?
▷ What furniture would they need?

Specification Checklist

✔ All designs must be based on the theme of Ancient Egypt.
✔ A range of designs for two and three-dimensional products is needed.
✔ The fabrics to be used will need to be...
✔ The fabrics will be printed by...
✔ The length of fabric needed will be...
✔ The number of colours will not be more than...

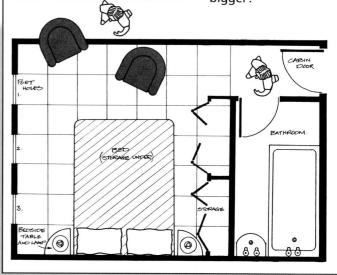

Spatial Planning

The cabin you will design measures 4 × 4 m square, excluding the bathroom. Using your understanding of scale and plan views, draw an outline and cut out the items of furniture you would expect to find in the cabin. Use these on an outline of the room space to work out where best to place them in relation to each other and to provide comfortable circulation through the space.

It might be helpful to draw the head and shoulders of an 'ergonome', so you can visualise the room in proportion to a scaled down person. Take into consideration access to and from the cabin and bathroom, i.e. opening doors, opening cupboard doors and the locality of the portholes.

Try various alternative room layouts and sketch your ideas, evaluating why you think one looks better than another.

Developing Ideas

From your original ideas you need to become more selective. Choose sample shapes and colours which you find interesting and you think will answer the brief.

You will need to produce a range of co-ordinated fabric designs for the following:

▷ two-dimensional textiles such as curtains, bed-spreads, carpets, wall-hangings, etc
▷ three-dimensional textile products such as lampshades and other furniture coverings, cushions, decorative wall hangings, etc
▷ wallpapers and borders.

Not all the fabrics need to be patterned. Some might be plain or textured.

Those which are patterned will need to contain a variety of pattern sizes and repeats, depending on what they are to be used for. Some might include a large image, e.g. Tutankhamun's death mask, while others might be based on a selection of hieroglyphics.

For each pattern design you will need to explore different colour variations, sometimes called colourways. Think carefully about which patterns go well with each other.

Remember to evaluate each design as you go, saying what you like and dislike about it.

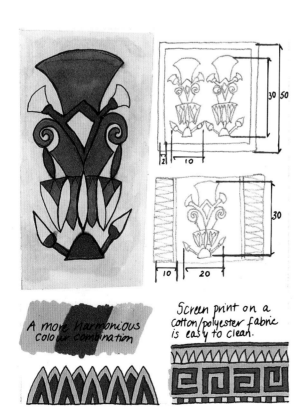

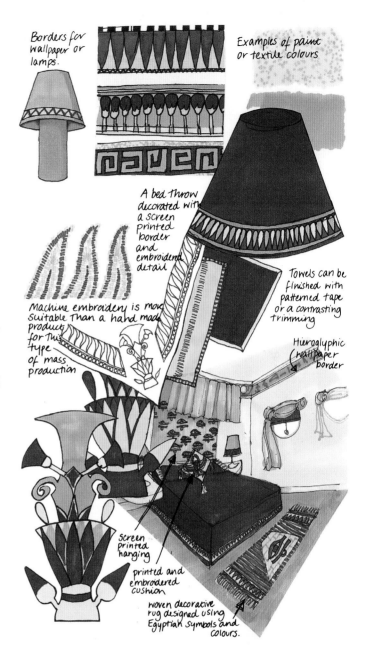

Finalising Your Ideas

As you develop your ideas further you will need to keep in mind what you know about:

▷ the most appropriate blends and mixes of fabrics
▷ fabric care
▷ the possibilities and limitations of printing.

Choose your most successful designs and refine them by working out the pattern size and repeat and the colourways in more detail and accuracy.

If you haven't already done so you need to decide which of your designs you are going to make up. It could be for either a two-dimensional or a three-dimensional textile product.

Specification/Developing Ideas: Logo and Uniform

Before beginning to design the uniform, focus on the limitations and possibilities of your design. You should have a clear idea of the corporate identity you want to create with your uniforms, and the specific requirements for one of the garments (e.g. a waistcoat).

To find out more about using CAD to design logos for garments go to:
www.gmd.org.uk

Designing the Logo

Logos should be simple and have an immediate impact. They often contain the name of the company or its initials.

▓ ACTIVITY

Make your own collection of examples of logos, particularly those of clothing manufacturers. Mount them in your project folder and evaluate them.
- ▶ What makes them effective?
- ▶ What message do they communicate about the company?

Work on the graphic aspects of the logo first – outlines and lettering.

Specification checklist

- ✔ The items of clothing which will make up the uniform will be...
- ✔ The impression/style they need to indicate will be...
- ✔ The range of sizes they will need to come in will be...
- ✔ The waistcoat is for...
- ✔ The print on the front must be...
- ✔ The materials will need to be...
- ✔ The colours will be...
- ✔ It must be comfortable to carry and convenient to use...
- ✔ The safety requirements are...
- ✔ The production cost will be...

Working in colour

Next work on colour variations – often referred to as **colourways** in industry.

Designers must balance the colours on a design so that one colour does not 'jump out' and break the continuity or harmony of the design. For example a T-shirt might be manufactured in four different colours. Colours for a screen print may work well with one background colour but may not harmonise with another. Pink and grey chosen for the print on a blue T-shirt may not work on a yellow one and therefore must be changed. It can be quite tricky to solve such problems.

Computer-aided design (CAD)

It may be possible to work on your logo designs with the help of a computer. Your school may have a computer-operated embroidery machine on which you could design and manufacture your logo. If not there may be draw/paint packages available to help you.

Developing Ideas

From your original ideas you need to become more selective. Choose sample styles, shapes and colours which you find interesting and you think will answer the brief.

You will need to produce ideas for a range of co-ordinated fabric designs for the range of garments you have identified for the uniform. Not all the fabrics need to be patterned. Some might be plain or textured.

Those which are patterned will need to contain a variety of pattern sizes and repeats, depending on what they are to be used for. Some might include a large image, e.g. Tutankhamun's death mask, while others might be based on a selection of smaller images, e.g. hieroglyphics.

For each pattern design you will need to explore different colourways. Think carefully about which patterns go well with each other.

Remember to evaluate each design as you go, saying what you like and dislike about it.

cotton/polyester side fastening waistcoat. Embellished with an embroidered scarab symbol

yellow cotton with screen printed design and contrasting

Heavy cotton twill is hard wearing and easy to care for.

Sweatshirt design for sports staff or a relaxed occasions

FRONT   BACK

Safari style jacket enforces the theme of exploration and is smart and practical. Can be worn with a skirt or trousers.

Short jacket with side fastening, could be worn by male staff with different shaping and a more 'boxy' shape.

Unisex trouser design

The jacket can be worn with an egyptian patterned scarf.

Patterned fabric designs suitable for shirts and scarves.

Luxor logo

Slim fitting jacket with matching skirt or trousers.

Alternative colours with contrasting piping down the front seam.

Finalising Your Ideas

As you develop your ideas further you will need to keep in mind what you know about:

▷ the most appropriate blends and mixes of fabrics
▷ fabric care
▷ the possibilities and limitations of printing

Choose your most successful designs and refine them by working out the pattern size and repeat and the colourways in more detail and accuracy.

If you haven't already done so you need to decide which of your designs you are going to make up into a finished garment to show to Luxor Travel.

Making it [1]: a Cushion

The next stage is to consider the design of the textile product (e.g. a cushion) you are going to make up as a sample.

You will then need to decide which way of printing your fabric best suits your design idea and to organise the correct equipment and the dyes you will require.

You will need to decide on the size, shape and pattern of your cushion design. Cushions can be any geometric shape including square, round, triangular, hexagonal etc., or organic, taking a more asymmetrical form e.g. a leaf, a squiggle, etc.

Side seam zip fastening

1 Measure the size of the zip fastening and mark its position centrally on the seam. Machine stitch along the seam from each corner to the marked points, then reverse about 1 cm to strengthen the ends.

2 Press the seam open. Place the zip on the wrong side, face down, centrally and tack into place.

3 Turn over to the right side and top stitch about 0.5 cm around the zip using a machine zip foot.

4 Remove tacking and finish off threads. With the zip slightly open, place the two sides of the cushion together, right sides facing, tack and complete as shown opposite.

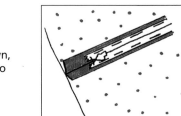

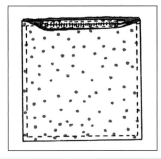

Making square covers

Square covers are the simplest to make. You must measure the size of your cushion pad, length and width ways, and add a **seam allowance** of 1 cm to each side.

1 Cut out two pieces of fabric this size for the front and back panels of your cushion. Remember to cut from the correct piece of fabric, especially if you want one side plain and the other patterned.

2 Place the right sides together (printed sides), with the edges matching. Pin, tack into place and machine stitch 1 cm from the edge. Remember to leave a central opening along one side for the cushion pad.

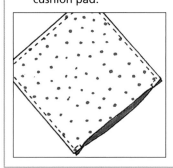

3 Finish off the beginning and ending of the machine stitching by reversing the stitch on the machine or by over sewing in the loose thread. Trim the seam allowances, snip across the corners, turn the cover the right way round and press with an iron.

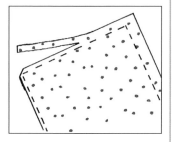

4 Insert cushion pad, turn in the raw edges in line with the seam and stitch the edges together.

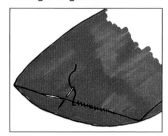

Making round covers

Measure the diameter of the pad and add 1 cm seam allowance. It may help to make a paper pattern of the circle. Proceed as for the square cover but when trimming, cut notches into the seam allowance at intervals to allow the seam to lie flat.

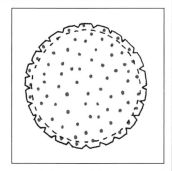

Embellishments

You may wish to use additional methods of embellishing fabrics to compliment your dying techniques in order to produce the finished design. Will the cushion be patterned on one or both sides, will it have a seamed, piped or ruffled edge?

Remember to decide which embellishments would be best applied before and after the construction of your cushion cover.

Decorative Edging

Ruffled edge

1 Decide on the width of the ruffle (usually 4 to 7.5 cm) and add 1 cm seam allowance. The length of the ruffle should be twice that of the outside edge measurement of the cushion.

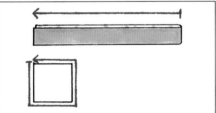

2 Hem the outer edge of the ruffle by turning it over twice at the edge and machine stitching.

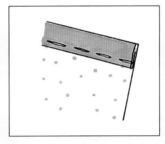

3 On the opposite edge run two rows of gathering stitches and gather in the ruffle to the desired length. Tack and stitch it into place. Complete the cushion as on the previous page.

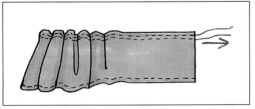

Pleated edge

For a pleated edge repeat as above but pleat the ruffle instead of gathering it.

Planning the Making

You will need to calculate how much fabric you will require. Ensure you print enough to include fabric waste and for any frills, etc., you have included in your cushion design.

Planning the Manufacturing

After you have made up your sample cushion you should think about manufacturing. You will need to prepare proposals for suitable methods of manufacturing the design in sufficient quantity and quality for *Luxor Travel*.

To help you do this, work through the following pages and decide how you could apply the various production and quality control methods to your design.

You may find that you need to suggest modifications to your designs to make them easier to manufacture.

Making it (2): a Waistcoat

A SEA CRUISE

Planning the manufacture of your garment will involve producing a pattern, cutting out the fabric and working out the order of making. You will need to draw up a production plan for each stage of manufacture. Include an equipment and materials list and a system for checking the quality of your work.

Pattern Adaption

You may have a **commercial pattern** which you can alter or use the diagram of the **block pattern** below and alter it to create the style of your design.

Test your pattern by making a model in paper or by sewing a sample from scrap fabric. Make any alterations necessary.

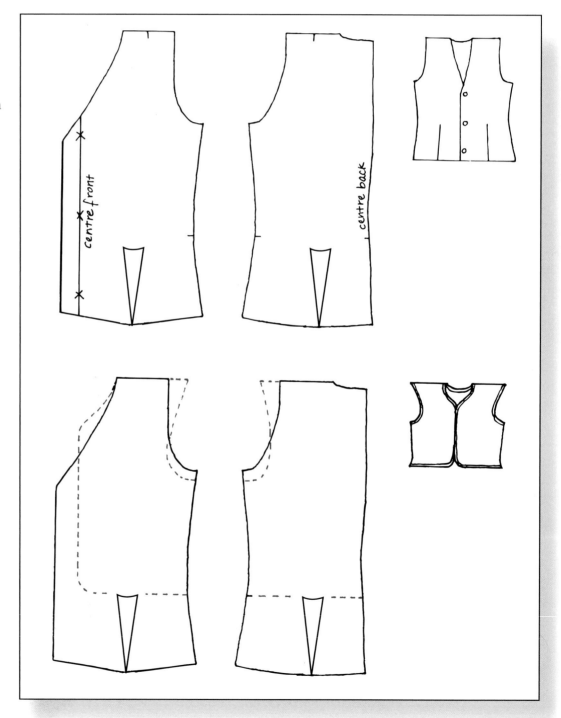

Adaptation

The following diagram shows how to alter your waistcoat in various ways.

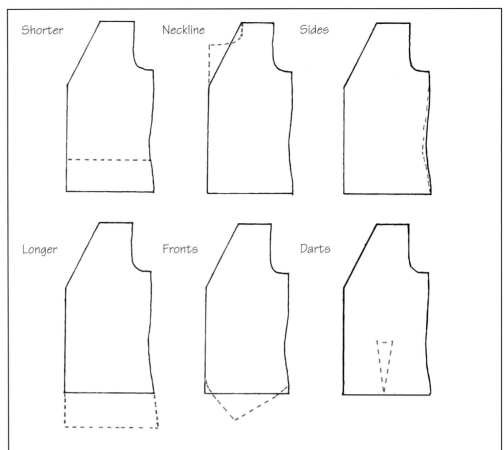

Planning the Manufacturing

After you have made up your sample waistcoat you will need to prepare your proposals for suitable methods of manufacturing the design in sufficient quantity and quality for *Luxor Travel*.

To help you do this, work through the following pages and decide how you could apply the various production and quality control methods to your design.

You may find that you need to suggest modifications to your designs to make them easier to manufacture.

Designing for Manufacture (1)

A SEA CRUISE

There are many different things that need to be considered when designing something suitable for manufacture. These include its life-expectancy, maintenance, and the need to reduce costs.

What do Textile Designers do?

Designers have to design within considerable constraints.

In the textile industries everything is driven by cost. It is a highly competitive industry both at home and abroad, so to succeed a manufacturer must produce the right goods for the right market at the right price. A designer must be fully aware of all aspects of production, not only the design stage, so that they can consider cost when they are designing.

Materials and labour are the biggest costs. The longer it takes to make an item the more expensive it will be. The same design can be made from differently priced materials. Designers must work with the available materials, components and production processes.

We needed a design which was easier, quicker and cheap to manufacture.

Before

▶ Pleated pockets with flaps
▶ Back and front yokes
▶ Double stitching on collar, cuff, front and back yokes, pockets and pocket flaps, front darts and hem
▶ 100% cotton/denim

Counting the costs

When a manufacturer is faced with a new product a major consideration has to be the way of keeping production costs to a minimum. Some elements will be **fixed costs** while others are known as **variable costs**.

Fixed costs are those incurred in setting up the production line such as machines, the tooling and factory space. Variable costs are likely to be the cost of materials, energy used, the wages of the workforce, insurance and maintenance, etc.

The costs of storage, transportation, packaging and selling all need to be taken into account as well.

The actual cost of the manufacturing of a product in terms of its materials and labour will vary according to the particular item. Often it only represents some 5-10% of the final selling price.

Manufacturers, wholesalers and retailers must make a profit. Many have to move abroad to reduce labour costs.

Design for life expectancy

Customers expect a certain minimum time that a product will last and one that fails before a reasonable time could be very costly for the manufacturer to repair, or in some cases replace.

If the customer's product shows early signs of wear and tear then they are unlikely to make a repeat purchase of the same brand and the brand might develop a reputation for being of poor quality.

However, if the product lasts for many years consumers will not need to buy replacements so often and demand will fall. The number of products that need to be manufactured will therefore drop and as a result the price may well rise. Many products therefore contain components that are likely to fail after a number of years and which would be very expensive to replace. This is called **planned obsolescence**.

Some textile products are designed and made to last longer than others. For example school jumpers and jeans are designed to be hard-wearing whereas an evening dress will not be worn as often and may go out of fashion so it does not need to be as hard-wearing.

A SEA CRUISE

manufacturing by design

■ ACTIVITY

How would you alter your product to make it more suitable for batch production and at a price suitable for your target market? Consider the following:
▶ the design of your product
▶ materials and components used
▶ techniques used
▶ machinery and production processes

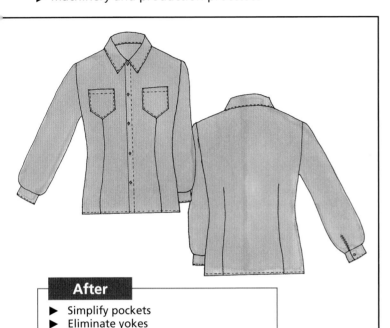

After
▶ Simplify pockets
▶ Eliminate yokes
▶ Use single stitching only
▶ Use light-weight denim

Design for Quantity

Products need to be designed to be easy to make. Some items may prove to be very difficult to make in quantity, however. This may be because of

▷ their shape
▷ techniques used on the design: anything very intricate which cannot be done by machine would be very time-consuming to make in quantity and therefore expensive.
▷ the way the components are placed
▷ the cost and availability of the materials required.

Different manufacturing processes and materials may need to be used according to the number being produced. A very expensive dress can be simplified and cheaper processes and materials can be used so it can be produced in quantity.

The rate of production can make a difference too, e.g.:

▷ 10,000 units by the end of next week
▷ 20,000 units over the next twelve months.

Design for maintenance

Designers have to consider how often a new product will need to be maintained during its usage, and take this into account while developing ideas. They will also have to think about how easy it will be to undertake the **maintenance** work. If a component needs cleaning, adjusting or replacing by the user, it must be quick and easy to do. (e.g. buttons are easier to replace than zips or press studs).

For example a uniform that is going to be worn every day must be easily laundered. It must be quick and easy to wash, dry and iron. If it needs dry cleaning it will be less practical.

Ideally a product should be virtually maintenance free, but this is likely to involve the use of higher quality fabrics, components and finer tolerances used in manufacture, which will inevitably increase the cost.

Design failures

Sometimes fashions fail because they are rejected by the public. Designers do not really dictate to the public what they should wear. They must be aware of current and future trends so that they can predict what will be acceptable.

There can be many reasons why a particular design is unsuccessful. Maybe noone wanted it because there was a better or cheaper alternative. Or perhaps it quickly became known that the product didn't wear well. Perhaps not enough money was invested in its promotion, with the result that many people just didn't know it was available, or weren't persuaded that they wanted or needed it. Possibly manufacturing costs proved to be much higher than expected, with the result that the company lost money, and had to cease production.

Finding fault

Much work goes into improving the design of an existing product. Companies often test their products using a variety of techniques to gather information and data so that direct comparisons can be made with other products.

Weaving tests may be carried out as well as fabric tests. Designs may be tested out in certain shapes to monitor the public's reaction to them. Feedback can be obtained through customer services departments within shops.

Sometimes a fault may not be with the original design but in the quality of manufacture.

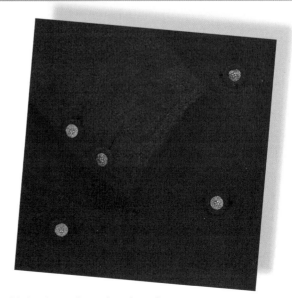

Self check wool suit by Chanel, 1960

Designing for Manufacture (2)

The world is a dangerous place. As designers and manufacturers produce new products, they need to ensure that they will be safe to use, and also safe to make.

Safe to Use

The designer must ensure that the product conforms to all the relevant safety standards, including those of other countries in which it might be sold. Careful consideration must be given to ways in which people might misuse the product, and any necessary safety devices and warning labels included: the designer can be held responsible for any accidents which occur as a result of poor design.

There are many laws in existence which help ensure that products are safe to use.

Safe to Make

It is the duty of an employer

'to ensure, as far as is reasonably practicable, the health, safety and welfare at work of all employees.'

(Health and Safety at Work Act, 1974)

There are four main areas to consider in order to help avoid potential accidents:

▷ the design of machinery and tools being used in the manufacturing process
▷ the physical layout of the work area
▷ the training of the workforce
▷ the safety devices and procedures.

In the manufacturing process there are a series of regulations and codes of practice which must be observed.

It is also essential to reduce the number of potential hazards – unsafe acts or conditions – which could occur in the workplace. Accidents are extremely costly in terms of personal distress, compensation and lost production.

Reducing the risks

Although we cannot avoid taking risks, we can take steps to assess the likelihood of something happening, and minimise its impact if it does.

As well as the legal requirements and more general codes of practice for Health and Safety, a considerable amount of documented information is available to help guide the design of safe products and working environments.

Ergonomic studies and anthropometric data can be used to determine optimum positions for displays and controls on products and machines, and the most suitable sizes and arrangements for work spaces and conditions (e.g. the distribution of light, noise, heating and ventilation).

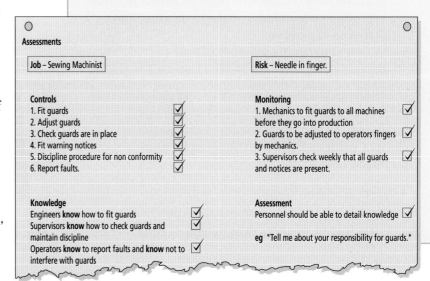

Design Issues

When specifying the requirements for a mass-produced product, designers need to consider a wide range of moral, economic, social, cultural and environmental issues. These often produce conflicts which can be hard to resolve.

Moral issues

In certain situations a product may have the capacity to injure or harm someone – either the user or a bystander. Cigarettes and alcohol are obvious examples. Bull bars on cars may look good and help improve sales, but they are likely to increase the severity of injury to a pedestrian in an accident.

Social issues

Some products can have a major impact on the way in which large groups of people live their lives. Convenience foods, for example, mean that there is less likelihood of the family sitting down together to eat a meal. Promotion and packaging can help counter this by providing two-person portions and using images of family meals.

Information and communication technologies are in the process of making a major impact on society, as work and shopping can be increasingly undertaken at home. Advanced automation reduces the number of people needed to produce and distribute goods, causing unemployment.

Cultural issues

The particular beliefs, ways of life and traditions of different groups of people have a major effect on the way they live their lives – what they do, where they go, and the things they buy.

Food and clothing and the symbolism of certain shapes and colours all play highly significant roles in maintaining the identity

of a particular culture. When a product is intended for use by a range of cultures it is important to identify and recognise such needs.

Risk assessment

When a production process involves hazardous situations it is necessary to analyse and assess each particular risk situation and ensure that adequate precautions are taken to minimise the potential danger.

It is the responsibility of an employer to assess the risks involved in each stage of production and justify the level of precautions adopted to a **Health and Safety Inspector**.

Once the risks have been identified they must be controlled and monitored. Below is an example of a **risk assessment** for a sewing machinist.

■ ACTIVITY

1. Design an ideal textiles working area for your school.

List all the tools and equipment needed.

Draw out a plan, positioning everything, taking into consideration safety and ergonomics.

2. Assess the risks involved in each stage of the production of one of the items you have designed and made. List all the employees for whom a risk assessment should be carried out. Use the example shown on the left to say how the risks can be reduced.

3. Carry out an investigation into the different attitudes to dress in your own and other cultures.

IN YOUR PROJECT

Make sure there are statements in your final production design report about:

► how much it will cost to make in quantity

► how long it might reasonably be expected to last without breaking or wearing out

► how frequently and easily different parts will need to be maintained

► aspects of the production which might be hazardous

► what steps you would recommend to be taken to minimise the risks, and why

► how moral, social and cultural issues have been considered.

119

Systems and Control

To design your product to be suitable for manufacture you need to know about the ways in which industrial production systems are organised.

Systems and Control

A **production system** is an interconnected series of events, materials and components. It is important for a designer to understand something about how such systems work together to make a product.

The role of a **production manager** is to establish how well a system is working and to find ways in which it could be improved, so that a product can be made more efficiently.

System boundaries

All systems are parts of an infinite number of larger and smaller systems. It is therefore essential to begin by defining the particular boundaries of the system to be studied. Supposing you wanted to study a factory production system. Are you going to consider the whole organisation which it is a part of, or just how efficiently one component is being made?

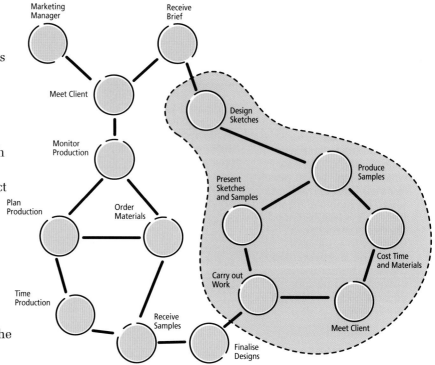

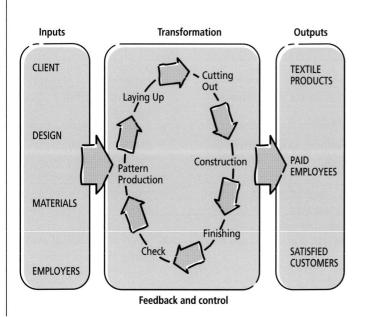

Inputs, outputs, and transformation processes

All systems have **inputs** and **outputs**. The main purpose of a system is to change or transform the inputs into outputs.

Most systems have many different sorts of inputs and outputs. The first stage in analysing a system is to identify the inputs, outputs and the **transformation processes** involved.

Again if we use a factory as an example of a system, the inputs might include raw materials, employees, manufacturing, equipment, energy, etc. The transformed outputs might include items of furniture, waste materials, paid employees, etc. The factory is a system for bringing such transformations about.

It is also possible to analyse a system in terms of a sequence of events, e.g. collect raw materials, prepare and mark them out, cut them, etc.

Feedback and control

Some transformation processes serve to maintain the equilibrium, or balance, of the system. Others work to improve the quantity and/or quality of the outputs.

It is possible to identify and analyse whether the various processes going on are maintaining the balance or attempting to improve quantity or quality.

When undertaking a **systems analysis** it might be discovered that the quantity or quality of the outputs are unsatisfactory in some way – too much waste material, or products which fail to meet the necessary quality specification and have to be thrown away.

As a result it may be found necessary to change the inputs, or to alter the process of transformation. This is known as **feedback**. The means by which the inputs or processes are changed are called **controls**.

The success of a system is judged by considering how well it transforms its inputs

into outputs, and how well it is prevented from failing to work satisfactorily as a result of its feedback and control mechanisms.

In the factory you might be examining the efficiency of a machine which bonds two surfaces together with an adhesive. It might be discovered that the acceptable limits of the amount of glue used are plus or minus 10%. Below this figure the surfaces will not stick adequately, and above the limit the manufacturing costs increase unacceptably.

The question then becomes how to ensure the machine works within these limits?

As well as quality of product or service provision, systems analysis often focuses on achieving acceptable production times.

Analysing a system involves looking at a complicated situation and being able to identify some degree of structure and connection between the things which are going on.

The pockets on our shirts are all crooked. Too much time is being spent on alterations in the pocket section – it is holding up the whole production line.

We collected data and analysed information about the system. We discovered that the stencils used to mark where the pockets should go on the front have not been cut completely straight. When the pockets are marked on using the stencil and chalk they are crooked

By correcting the stencil and ensuring that the chalk marks are in the right position – the machinist can stitch the pockets on straight.

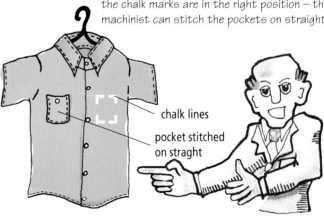

chalk lines

pocket stitched on straght

Undertaking a systems analysis

STAGE 1
Identify and clearly state:

▶ the main inputs and outputs of the system.
▶ which specific inputs and/or outputs you are interested in investigating (i.e. which you suspect to be unsatisfactory in some way)
▶ the parts of the feedback and control operations which need to be investigated (i.e. which you suspect to be un-satisfactory in some way)

STAGE 2
The next step is to collect as much information as possible about the way in which the parts of the system you are interested in works. This may involve collecting factual information (e.g. how long or how often something takes to happen) and opinions (people's observations and comments). In particular you need to try to find out:

▶ what happens when things don't run smoothly, or in an emergency
▶ how the system is maintained over different periods of time.

STAGE 3
Finally, evaluate the extent to which:

▶ the transformation process is over complicated and wasteful
▶ the limits of the feedback system (i.e. the points at which mechanical adjustments or decisions for action are made) are too high or too low

▶ suitable provisions have been made for emergency operation and maintenance
▶ the system can be easily modified to take account of later needs
▶ various changes in the original inputs to the system would improve its performance.

Production Process Systems (1)

A SEA CRUISE

The quicker and easier it is to make something, the more can be made and therefore the cheaper it becomes. This makes the product available to a greater number of people.

What method of production will you be using?

Production Methods

One-off production

One highly skilled craftsperson may produce a single garment over days or weeks. The time taken will depend on the design of the garment and the techniques used to create it. For example a hand-beaded dress will take considerably longer than a simple T-shirt.

One-off production may be used in the theatre where only one costume is required for a specific character.

It is also used by a fashion house wanting to produce a garment to fit an individual customer. This is very costly in terms of labour and materials and only a very small number of people can afford to buy such garments, but these garments are finished to a very high quality.

Art textiles such as wall hangings and creative embroidery are also 'one-offs'.

Batch production

When a specified number of identical items have to be produced a team of people can make them in less time than one person working on their own. The team share tasks and equipment and may become particularly skilled at one or more of the operations involved in the production of the item. Working this way allows for some flexibility so that they can respond quickly to changes in market demand by switching to making a different design. One week they might make a batch of 10,000 T-shirts of one design, and the next switch to making 5,000 units of a completely different design.

Mass production

If a number of workers work on a production line they can each do one part of the manufacturing process before passing the product onto the next person. This enables them to make identical products very quickly eight or more hours a day for weeks or months on end.

Although this significantly reduces time and costs, the whole production quickly halts if there is a problem, and changing the line to make a different product can take a long time.

This method is not necessarily used in clothing manufacture as styles change often. However, some factories may specialise in a few 'classic' products (e.g. jeans, socks, etc) so that the production system can be designed to permanently manufacture them. Using this method it is possible to produce a pair of jeans in 10 minutes.

Fabrics which are needed constantly may be mass-produced, e.g. plain weave cotton. Most production processes involve a mixture of these methods. Some parts might need to be individually or batch produced, while others will be run off continuously.

Different types of manufacturing equipment are needed for the different processes. Some require special purpose tools made to suit a particular product, while others require basic machines with parts which can be changed and re-programmed when needed.

Standardised Design

In many industries a basic **standardised design** is produced to maximise on the economies of large-scale production. Different components, features and accessories, and finishes are then added to the basic design to produce a range to offer the customer

Some styles of clothing stay basically the same, such as shirts and trousers. Only the style details such as pockets, colour and shape may change. This means that a manufacturer can organise production for the manufacture of a basic garment but retain enough flexibility to alter the shape of the pockets, etc.

Standardised Production

Many fabrics (such as plain woven cotton) which are constantly in demand are woven continuously, and then dyed and printed in different patterns and colourways.

In fabric printing silk screens and rollers are used to produce lengths of identical pattern repeats over and over again (see pages 104 to 107).

Pattern lays allow many pieces to be cut at the same time.

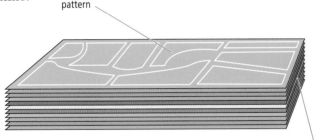

pattern

fabric layers

Specialised machinery

As well as using machines which can carry out many different functions, highly specialised machines are used to carry out identical operations which need to be repeated many times. These include automatic dart sewers, buttonholers, hemming units, automatic patch pocket setters, pocket flap-sewing machines, etc.

KEY POINTS

- Most production processes are based on a combination of one-off, batch and mass production.
- Special machines are used to make identical parts or stitches.

Production Process Systems (2)

A SEA CRUISE

It is possible to define the step by step process by which most products are going to be made in simple terms. The different stages of manufacture can then be grouped together into key areas of production.

This flow chart shows the key stages in the production of a waistcoat

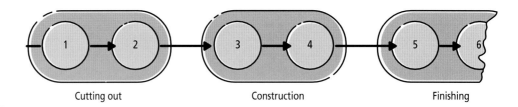

Cutting out   Construction   Finishing

When planning a production line, different types of operations are coded by using standard symbols.

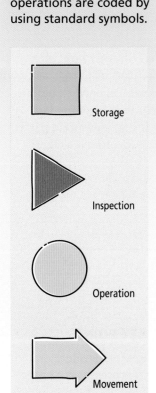

Storage

Inspection

Operation

Movement

Planning a Production Stage in Detail

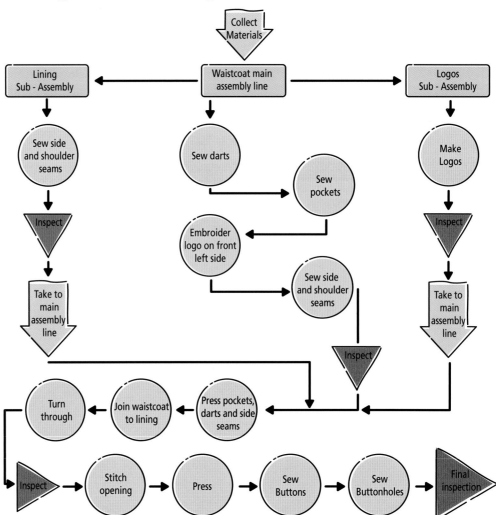

Sub-assemblies

When all the operations have been identified, the next stage is to plan the layout of the **production line**. This is likely to involve a number of **sub-assemblies**, where groups of component parts are assembled before they are added into the main production line. For example the embroidered logo on the waistcoat may be in the form of a badge which has been manufactured elsewhere, bought in by the waistcoat manufacturer and either fused or stitched on.

Sub assemblies are often made in what are called manufacturing cells. These are smaller individual units where four or five people operate specific machines or assemble items. Manufacturing cells are now frequently used in the British clothing industry as the workers can build up a range of skills on different operations. This makes the work-force more flexible, which is important for the production of smaller numbers of high quality garments aimed at a smaller market.

Another way of organising a manufacturing process involves grouping similar machines and/or materials together in one area. This has some advantages, but generally increases the distances that components need to travel.

It is important to ensure that the correct materials and components arrive at the production line at exactly the right time and place. Many factories use a production control system called 'just in time' to ensure this happens in the most efficient way.

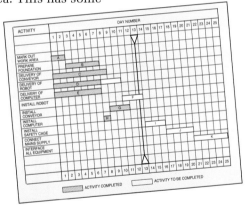

A Gannt chart

In all types of production, a complex and accurate production schedule is essential to tell everyone when to prepare, assemble and finish the different components.

CAD-CAM CASE STUDY

Birds Eye Walls

Factory layouts and production scheduling can now be efficiently done using computer-based systems.

The Birds Eye Walls CAD system has the power to allow you to fly through three-dimensional views of the factory and see how new layouts will look in practice. Production machines are built up on screen as a series of blocks. These can be moved round quickly to see where they fit best.

Layers (like sheets of tracing paper) are used within the CAD package to hold the details of different services such as water, steam, air and chemicals.

The system is much more accurate than old methods of drawing. Although the initial CAD drawing takes just as long to produce, a great deal of time is saved when changes are made because a completely new drawing is no longer needed each time.

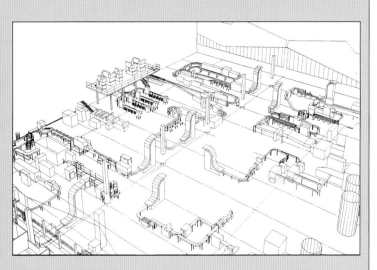

Computer-aided Design (CAD)

CAD systems make it easy to create a picture of a new design, and then to change the way it looks on the screen. This means that new ideas or variations on an idea can be tried out and evaluated much more quickly than if they had to be redrawn each time.

There are a number of different types of CAD program available. Some are more concerned with the visual appearance of a product, others with technical detail.

Computers have become an integral part of the design, colour and repeat process. They can dramatically cut down on labour and time, and therefore costs.

However designers still need to have an understanding of traditional design aesthetics and hand-painting. The computer is a tool, it will not make design judgements for you.

Computer systems contain three main elements – a series of **inputs** which are **transformed** into **outputs**.

CAD can speed up the entire design, manufacture and retail process. The more new styles you get in the store, the more sales you can generate. Some stores want new styles on the floor every month so they can have maximum newness.

Input	Transformation	Output
A motif or design can be scanned into the computer. It is then ready to be altered.	The computer can make many different repeats and colour combinations very quickly.	Presentation boards giving a good idea of what fabric will look like on a range of garments.

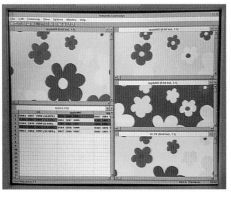

Image mapping allows a textile design to be draped on a figure in seconds and shows exactly what the final garment will look like draped on a model. Previously the designer would have had to make up the garment to see what it looked like.

Methods of Representation

There are three main ways of representing an object on a computer.

▷ **wire-frame modelling** means that the object is represented by a series of lines. This image can be enhanced by removing lines that would be hidden.

▷ **surface modelling** can be added. The surfaces of the object are represented by colour, shading and texture to give a stronger sense of three-dimensional form.

▷ **solid modelling** where the drawing is based on geometrical shapes which can be mathematically analysed.

Transforming a CAD model

Most CAD programs have certain common facilities. Drawing tools produce lines which can be adjusted for width, shape and colour and can be set to produce curved lines as well. The designer is also able to access a library of existing images which can be added to a design.

It is very easy to transform a CAD drawing or image by copying, rotating and mirroring different parts of it. These functions are usually available on an on-screen menu.

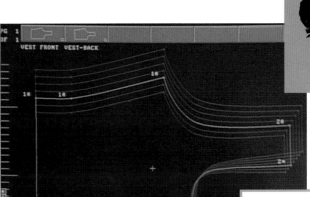

The Impact of ICT

Computers are also used to help develop new materials. Special programs can predict the precise physical properties and the performance of new combinations of fibres and finishes.

Du Pont, for example, have recently developed a new bullet and knife-resistant material. Using a computer they were able to predict how far different possible materials would be penetrated and the shape of the indentation. This helped them solve the problem of designing something which achieved the right balance between the effectiveness of the material at absorbing impact and its bulk and weight, which can make it cumbersome and uncomfortable to wear.

IN YOUR PROJECT

Depending on which packages you have at school, CAD could be used to:

▶ create a 3D surface-textured drawing of your idea
▶ produce detailed working drawings
▶ work out the arrangement of pattern pieces that can be obtained from the original fabric.

KEY POINTS

The key advantages of using CAD are:

● it speeds up the process of design development, and as a result a greater variety of designs can be produced.

● an improvement in the quality of design, because the computer can more accurately simulate and produce accurate information about how the design will behave in different operating conditions.

● any changes can be made quickly and communicated throughout the team working on the project.

● design information which has been generated can be stored in a database or file and can be quickly and easily retrieved at a later date.

A SEA CRUISE

products and applications

Computer-aided Manufacture (CAM)

A SEA CRUISE

An increasing number of production processes can now be done by machines which are controlled by computers. Automated manufacturing is safer, quicker, more reliable, and in the long run, cheaper.

  ICT

Making it by computer

CAM is a term used to describe the process whereby parts of a product are manufactured by equipment that is controlled by a computer.

One of the restrictions of batch-production is that after a relatively small number of products have been made a machine has to be re-set to the requirements of a different product.

The main advantage of CAM is that the new instructions are stored electronically and can be down-loaded and programmed into the machine very quickly. This also facilitates making small changes to the design to suit changes in the market or to

produce specialised short-run products for individual clients. Where **computer-aided manufacture** is used to replace a manual operation, greater productivity is possible, because the machine can work continuously. There is also a greater consistency of quality, and fewer faulty goods. CAM systems can also work with materials and chemicals which might be harmful to human operators.

In many cases the manufacture of a complete product is a combination of CAM and hand operations. An example of this may be where the cutting and machining of a panel is completed using the CAM facility but the application of a suitable finish is done by an operator.

Computer numerical control (CNC)

Computer numerically controlled (CNC) machine tools can be independently programmed, but also have the facility to transfer data to other computers. They therefore become part of a complex automated production system. This is particularly effective where a number of smaller manufacturers specialise in the making of a component which contributes to a whole product.

Computer integrated manufacture (CIM)

CAD and CAM systems contribute to the development of computer integrated manufacture (CIM). This is a totally automated production process with every aspect of manufacture controlled by computer.

Powerful CAD systems can be linked into a CIM system. This allows the entire design development, production schedule and manufacturing operation to be undertaken by a single system.

Manufacturing companies which have adopted such systems have been able to make dramatic reductions in the production costs of their products, and increase their quality and reliability.

Making it Somewhere Else

New ways are being developed of creating and sending information electronically.

Computer-generated data about a final design can be sent almost anywhere in the world in a few seconds. The data is then fed directly from the computer into manufacturing equipment to make the product.

CAD-CAM in Action

Clothing

Patterns can be drafted and graded on a computer using computer-aided design (CAD) and then produced to the full-size using a plotter. Lays can be planned on the computer which can then quickly work out the percentage wastage of fabric created by the use of that lay. This was previously an extremely time-consuming process.

Using numerical control the cutter can then be programmed to cut round each pattern piece on the lay.

Eighty per cent of the time required for garment assembly goes on handling component pieces. This time can be reduced using robotic devices. Programmable sewing and embroidery machines and garment presses also speed the manufacturing process up considerably.

Textiles

After a design has been created, a **CAD-CAM system** can make the colour separations which can be saved on a disc. The disc can be sent to the mill and the printers can use the information to engrave the screens. This eliminates any translation from the artist's design concept to the final printed fabric.

The computer interfaces with a larger engraver at the mill which will then print the fabric. The quality assurance built into this technique eliminates the time and expense of having a stylist at the mill supervising the printing of samples.

Colour matching, and the weighing and dispensing of chemicals and dyes can be done automatically by computer. All the production data concerning the materials used, work in progress, quality checks and finished work can be monitored and stored by a computer for later analysis.

Ancient and modern are woven together

Nicholas Booth reports on ScotWeave, the design system that has brought the traditional loom into the 21st century.

Computer technology has taken the ancient craft of weaving and designing fabrics into a new realm that is faster, cheaper and more accurate than ever before. Designs can be realised in a matter of hours rather than days and at a fraction of the cost.

The traditional design process in weaving has changed little since the invention of the loom.

It was often long and involved with patterns fashioned using coloured squares and then translated by punch card into final instructions on the loom. Often the designers didn't know how the finished product would look. It used to take six months from design to woven fabric. Now it's five minutes.

As you enter its workshops a Polaroid photograph of you will be taken; by the time you leave after being shown around, you will be presented with a piece of fabric with that image woven into it – a very graphic demonstration of the power of the technology.

The CAD package can produce all types of design on to any material – multi-section blankets, complex weave structures or even kaleidoscopic patterns. Sixteen million colours can be defined and brought up on the screen. If a customer has a particular colour in mind they can incorporate it into the design. A spectrophotometer is used to measure accurately the colours of yarn and dye samples for precise matching. The data is fed directly into the system and the colour is reproduced exactly.

Source: *The Times*, 1996

Quality Counts

A SEA CRUISE

Manufacturers need to ensure that all the products they are producing are of an acceptable standard. A range of techniques has been developed to help check and maintain quality over a long production run.

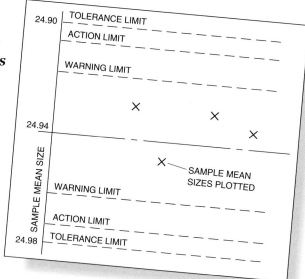

Working to a Tolerance

As you have probably discovered it is difficult making something accurately. In complex products a high degree of accuracy is essential to ensure that all the parts fit together exactly. The important question is how accurate does it need to be? This will vary according to the requirements of the product.

The answer to this question is known as the **tolerance level** – the extent to which the size of a component must be accurate. This is usually expressed by two numbers: an upper and lower limit.

In a simple example, a skirt intended to be 24 cm in length could vary between 23.5 cm and 24.5 cm. The tolerance is the difference between the upper and lower limits, i.e. 1 cm, or + or – 5 mm.

New automated equipment tends to be quicker and more efficient at producing and testing components which are finely toleranced. The higher the degree of accuracy, the better the quality of the product.

Achieving this greater accuracy requires careful measurement and skill in controlling tools. This usually means that the cost will be higher.

Testing procedures are needed to ensure items are within the stated tolerance levels. These are usually set by the manufacturer, but in some cases they will be set by the client.

Quality Control Systems

One way to check the quality of products as they are made is to check every one to ensure that each is satisfactory. A more sophisticated and quicker approach is to set up a system of **quality control**. This involves inspecting a sample of components as they are made, and the gathering and analysing of records of the samples.

Defects can be rated, for instance:

▷ critical – signifies an almost certain customer complaint
▷ major – a basic sewing fault
▷ minor – almost trivial and the customer probably would not even notice.

In simple terms, a sample of components (say 1 in every 100) are subjected to rigorous tests which identify and record how close the item is to its target. Provided it is found to be within acceptable limits, production continues.

By examining the pattern of a series of tests it may be possible to notice that a particular machine is increasingly producing components which are getting close to the un-acceptable tolerance limits.

In such a situation it is possible to adjust, or if necessary repair, the machine before it starts to produce items which would have to be classed as defective and possibly shut-down the production line. The aim of quality control is therefore to achieve zero defects by predicting the failure of a machine before it happens.

The use of automated testing machines and of electronic gathering and analysis of data leads to higher standards of quality and less wastage.

Quality Assurance

Quality assurance is the overall approach that ensures high standards of quality throughout the company. It includes the development and monitoring of standards, procedures, documentation and communications across the company as a whole. Usually a quality manual is produced which contains all the relevant information to guide staff.

British Standards

One of the major bodies that promotes quality is the **British Standards Institute**. They produce documents that clarify the essential technical requirements for a product, material or process to be fit for its purpose. There are over 10,000 British Standards for almost every industry from food to building construction and textiles to children's toys.

Certification that a product conforms to a stated British or European Standard provides an assurance that an acceptable quality can be expected. This reduces the risk of someone buying a product which could be defective in some way.

Critical control checks

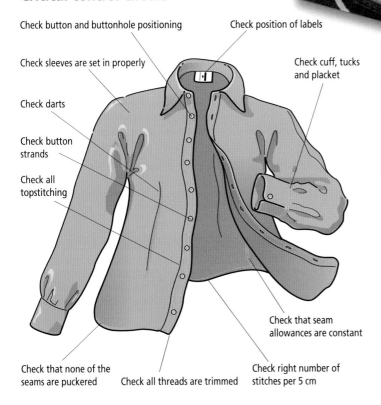

Check button and buttonhole positioning

Check sleeves are set in properly

Check darts

Check button strands

Check all topstitching

Check position of labels

Check cuff, tucks and placket

Check that seam allowances are constant

Check that none of the seams are puckered

Check all threads are trimmed

Check right number of stitches per 5 cm

Quality costs
Costs can be incurred:

▶ in the design, implementation, operation and maintenance of quality management systems.
▶ owing to failures of the systems or products.

Reliability
The success of a product depends on how reliable it is in use. Reliability is an important element of **quality management** and must be designed and planned into products and services.

Testing whether a design functions well is possible but it is often difficult, sometimes impossible to test a product for reliability.

Designers and manufacturers can do their best to ensure reliability by considering the following:

▶ the use of proven designers
▶ use of the simplest possible design (this lowers the chance of failure)
▶ use of fabrics, trimmings and equipment likely to perform well.
▶ specifying proven production methods.

Catalogue 2001

Products and Services

IN YOUR PROJECT

▶ How accurately do the different parts of your design need to be made?
▶ Which components need to fit together most accurately?
▶ Identify the best time to check for accuracy.
▶ What type of testing is to be carried out?
▶ How often do you need to complete these checks?
▶ Which British Standards would apply to the production of your design?

KEY POINTS

● The specification for a product should include a statement about its tolerance limits.
● Tolerances are important to ensure reliability, which in turn reduces wastage of products during manufacture.
● Testing procedures are needed to ensure items are within the stated tolerance limits.
● Quality control systems help manufacturers reduce wastage and delay in production. They do this by predicting failure or other potential problems before they happen.
● Quality control production checks form a specific part of a broader programme of quality assurance across a company.

Back to Badges

You have decided that the company logo for the crew of the the Gift of the Nile will be made up as fabric badges. You need to work out how four different coloured batches of twenty five badges can be manufactured quickly and cheaply.

Work together in groups of four, and remember, teamwork counts!

Developing the Design

You will need to have finalised your idea for the logo design and worked out how the badge will be made.

The design work to this point should not be included in the timing of the production process simulation.

Developing the Production Sequence

1 Devise a flow-process chart which identifies the various main stages in:

▶ preparing the materials (e.g. making sure there is a steady supply of materials which are ready to use when required)
▶ making the badges
▶ checking the quality .

You will also need to decide how to organise the work space (i.e. where tools and materials will be placed for easy access).

2 To begin with, just one of you should make a single badge from start to finish, with the other members of the team timing how long it takes and thinking about how it might be possible to organise the production line more effectively.

3 Next focus on each separate stage and consider how the work might be divided up. Some possibilities are:

▶ each person works in line, passing on a partly completed product to the next person
▶ on some stages, two or more people work together

▶ some people may have more than one job at different parts of the process.

4 It is also important to design the most efficient organisation of the work space – i.e., where materials and workers will be best placed to minimise delays in moving partly-completed products around. Storage space and location is also important to consider.

5 Another key consideration is how the different colour variations will be organised. For example would it be better to make them continuously or in batches of different colours?

6 How might specially-made jigs or templates help to speed things up?

7 It is essential that you make products which are of a good quality. Define tolerances for the badges. What effect would different tolerances make to the quality and cost of the badges? Where and how will you build in quality control checks? Devise a quality specification for some of the operations.

8 Experiment with a variety of arrangements of production layouts and scheduling until the most effective is identified. To achieve this you will need to work closely together and co-operate well.

Group discussion and decision-making meetings are essential. At these sessions you might like to consider taking on specific roles of responsibility for various aspects of the process, e.g. stock control, quality control, work flow.

Agree and organise the final layout and obtain the necessary stock of card etc., to prepare for the final test simulation run.

The design and development of the production process to this point should not be included in the timing of the final simulation run.

9 Run your production process simulation. Time how long it takes. Count how many badges are below an acceptable quality standard. Work out the cost of manufacturing.

Flow Chart for making badges

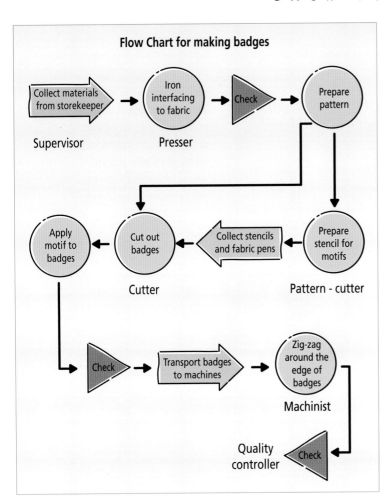

Design and Make It Better!

Whether your production design turns out to be the most efficient at the end of the run is not the end of the exercise, however. The next question is how can it be improved further to increase quality and reduce costs.

From what you now know about production, go back to review the original design and manufacture of the badges.

▷ Did you choose the best methods of production?
▷ Would adding extra members into the team make a worthwhile difference to the production-rate?
▷ If a much longer production run was planned, how would the schedule and layout need to be developed?
▷ What parts of the process could be most effectively automated?

Write up a report of the project, including graphs and charts and diagrams to illustrate the different layouts and schedules used.

Costing your badges

You will need to work out the cost of producing the different coloured badge designs in batches of 25. It is always more economical to produce in bulk rather than individual items as materials and trimmings can be bought in bulk.

In industry **overheads** need to be included in the manufacturing cost. These include things like equipment, factory space, and energy. Add 10% to the costs of your materials to represent the costs of 'overheads'.

Labour costs make up a large percentage of the manufacturing cost. Calculate your own labour costs, based on your production simulation. Work to a rate of £5 per hour per worker. (This includes 'add-on' costs such as National Insurance and administration.)

When costing the materials and components for your badges remember that the costs are reduced as you use more.

	Amounts used	Cost (£)
Materials	100 cm at £2.90 per metre	0.29
Threads		1.00
Interfacing		0.20
Dyes / paints	Various	1.00

After the first 50 metres the cost of the material drops to £2.30 per metre. After the next 100 metres the cost of the material drops to £1.99 per metre.

- *Threads can be priced per reel or amount used per design*
- *Interfacing is priced per metre and the price also goes down depending on amount used*
- *Dyes and paints will be costed as per pot*

Green Textiles

A SEA CRUISE

> *'The air, the water, the soil are not a gift from our parents but a loan from our children'*
>
> Haida tribe of North American Indians

Environmentalism became a very important issue in recent years. In textiles design the materials themselves and the processes used to produce them all have an impact on the environment.

To find out more about recycling and sustainability go to:
www.ethicalconsumer.org
www.greenchoices.org
www.ethicalexchange.co.uk
www.greenshop.co.uk
www.naturalcollection.com
www.greenfibres.co.uk

It is important to realise that there is no such thing as a completely 'green' manufactured product. However it is possible to make 'greener' products by introducing clean technologies to replace polluting processes, by careful selection of raw materials and by reducing the amount of energy and water used during manufacture.

This coat is entirely recycled wool, shredded, respun into yarn and woven back into new cloth

Dyeing

The biggest environmental problems involved in the textile dyeing processes are the vast amounts of water consumed and the transfer of dye into the effluent. This results in a pollutant that is unsightly, often toxic and not quickly biodegradable. New processes are presently being developed which do not pollute the effluent and which keep water consumption to a minimum.

Legislation

As well as trying to meet the demand for greener products the textile and clothing industry is being put under increasing pressure to clean up its act by both UK and European Commission legislation. It is important however to create balance by providing protection for Europe's conscientious companies so that they do not find themselves overcome by cheaper competition from countries where no environmental legislation applies. While new processes involve an initial increase in capital investment, the reduction of expenditure on waste and energy should eventually lead to greater efficiency.

Is natural always best?

In response to consumer demand many clothing companies have made sweeping claims about the greenness of their products. High profile marketing campaigners have promoted the myth that 'natural is best' while the synthetics market suffers from the negative image of the chemical companies with which they are associated. However cotton is environmentally unsound for a number of reasons:

▶ it is one of the major users of pesticides on a world scale
▶ it takes up valuable crop growing land in areas like India and Pakistan.

Cotton production processes such as mercerizing, bleaching and dyeing harm the environment. Cotton garments need higher washing and ironing temperatures than synthetics

Organic and naturally coloured cotton are scarce and much more expensive than the conventional kind. It is likely to remain a very small market as growing conditions limit production, although growth in demand would go some way towards spurring production and bringing prices down.

Eco-labelling

This is a scheme being piloted by the EC on T-shirts and bed-linen in Denmark. Products must pass a stringent set of criteria before they can be deemed worthy of carrying the eco-label. The criteria examine key features of the product in all stages of its life-cycle. These include energy consumption, consumption of water, and pesticides used during cotton growing and sheep rearing. It is expected that companies will want to meet these high standards in order to gain access to a growing green consumer market.

The 'cradle to grave' approach

Eco-labelling is an example of this approach. It means judging the 'greenness' of a product right through its entire life-cycle.

```
Raw materials
    ↓
Manufacturing processes
    ↓
Energy consumption
in production  →  Transport
                      ↑
                  Packaging
                      ↑
              Use of the product
              by the consumer
                      ↑
              Environmental impact
              of product disposal
              after use
```

Fabrics from Recycled Bottles

A high performance fibre called Trevira Two can now be recycled from plastic bottles. It is intended that the fabric will be used in high performance outdoor garments and sportswear. The manufacturers believe that if recycled products are really going to make an impact on the economy and the environment, then they must meet consumer expectations aesthetically and in quality and performance. The fabric, which contains 50% post-consumer polyester and is indistinguishable from virgin polyester, has the following environmental benefits.

▶ Reduction of waste
▶ Reduction of landfills
▶ Reduces the amount of virgin fabric that needs to be manufactured.

Textile Recycling

The recycling of woollen textiles into a fibre form suitable for re-spinning has been an industry in England for about 200 years, started by Samuel Law in Yorkshire.

Today **textile recycling** has expanded but it is still on a small scale compared to other recycling industries such as glass and paper.

The chart below shows the break-down of the end products that might typically be produced from 100 kg of discarded textiles.

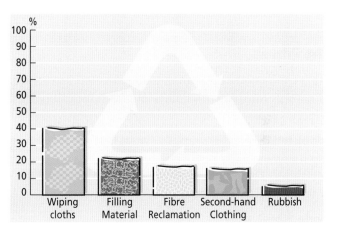

Up to 1 million tonnes of old textiles end up in rubbish tips and landfills every year but 95% of this would be suitable for reclaiming.

The industry can only expand to meet demand. To create a demand customers have to be persuaded to buy recycled textiles. Textile banks may increase public interest in this area of recycling in the future.

■ ACTIVITY

▶ Find out more about textile recycling in your local area?
▶ Which textile products used at home or at school could be easily recycled?

KEY POINTS

● Environmental issues are a particular concern of the textile industry.
● As well as legislation there needs to be a demand by the consumer for green products.

IN YOUR PROJECT

▶ Consider ways in which each stage of manufacture of your product could be made greener.
▶ Develop a specification for an eco-label for your product.

Tomorrow's Textiles Today

A SEA CRUISE

The pressure to develop cheaper, more versatile and environmentally acceptable materials is producing a variety of exciting new fibres and fabrics.

WWW.

If you want to find out about synthetic fibres and fabrics such as Coolmax, Tactel and Kevlar go to:
www.Dupont.com
www.nexia.com
www.Speedo.com

Plant Fibres

There have recently been attempts to develop fabrics from natural sources which have not been traditionally or widely used.

Pineapple fibre

These fibres have a translucent quality and an almost glassy shine. They do not take up coloured dye well, so tend to be used as interlining.

Banana fibre

Banana fibres have a long history of village production, but now clothes industrially made from banana products are becoming available. The fabric is thin, matt and opaque, rather like raffia. Again it is used for interlining.

Ramie

The ramie shrub is a member of the nettle family. It has a life span of 30 years and can be cropped three times a year, making it an environmentally sound fabric. Ramie is usually mixed with polyester and/or acrylic to give it a crushproof linen look.

Skins

Salmon skin

Salmon skins have recently been used as a serious alternative to leather for smaller items, such as shoes. Each skin has individual markings and there are claims that it is actually stronger than leather. The skins are a by-product of the Scottish smoked-salmon industry.

New Fibres

Textile technologists endeavour to improve existing fibres and fabrics and to develop new ones.

Tencel

Tencel (hi-tenacity cellulose) is the first new fibre to be developed for 30 years and has become very popular. It feels like silk and breathes like cotton but has none of the drawbacks of either.

Tencel is produced by Courtaulds Fibres who pride themselves on its environmental friendliness because it is made from wood pulp from sustainable forests. What little waste the production process leaves is non-hazardous.

The fibre appeals to leading designers such as Katharine Hamnett as well as to popular high street stores.

Many of the garments are machine washable and hold their colour well because the fibres are absorbent.

They cost little more than similar garments made from cotton and do not crease as much as linen.

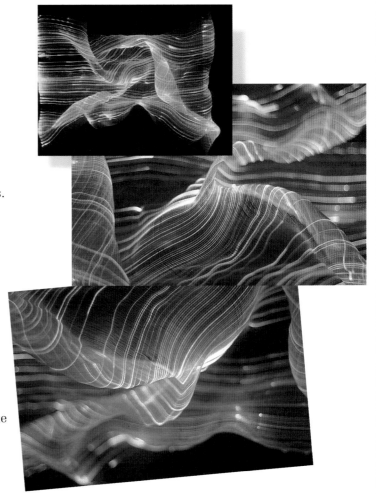

Technological Textiles

Recent developments in textiles technology include:

▷ metallic colours
▷ dyes which are sensitive to light
▷ improved methods of bonding metals on to yarns or cloth.

Biominetics is the process of creating new fibres which work in a similar way to nature. For example **Stomatex** emulates the way in which a pinecone opens and closes. **Fastskin**, the fabric designed for all in one swimming costume, is based on the texture of sharkskin and how sharks move through water.

Other new technological developments include **Thermochromatic** printing inks, which react to heat and change colour depending on the temperature, and **Microencapsulation** – the process by which scents and fragrances and other ingredients can be added to fabrics. Another new fibre is called **Bio-Steel**. This is made from the casein of goats milk, and is very strong and also recyclable.

It is possible to create fabrics which change colour as the viewer moves around the room. The fabric is laminated with a fine plastic film embossed with tiny lenses that refract different areas of pattern as the viewer moves.

Another process involves adding a chemical to a length of cloth which can be printed on and then baked at high temperature to burn away patterns with fine detail. This creates a cheaper alternative to lace.

A different effect can be achieved by applying acids to cloth which elongates it, making blistered and puckered surfaces.

Microfibres

Microfibres are produced by mixing polymers to produce fibres that are even finer than silk. They are mostly made from polyester, but nylon and acrylic are sometimes used, and they can be blended with other fibres such as cotton. The fabrics they are made into retain and extend the properties of the fibres from which they have been made. Depending on the properties which are needed the microfibres can be woven or knitted.

Microfibres can be woven so closely together they can prevent water from permeating, but as they also have high moisture transference properties they still allow perspiration to escape. They are used for items such as lens-cloths and weather-proof fabrics for various outdoor activities. Microfibre cloth hangs well and is extemely soft, lightweight, durable and comfortable to wear.

■ ACTIVITIES

▶ Find out more about recent developments in textile technologies. Write letters to manufacturers and look up newspaper and magazine articles with up-to-date information.

KEY POINTS

● Textile technology is constantly evolving to meet new demands, improve existing products and solve environmental problems.
● New developments include the use of natural, synthetic and microfibres.

A SEA CRUISE

products and applications

The Future of Fashion

www.

A SEA CRUISE

The clothing and textile industry needs to constantly keep changing to take account of new materials, new manufacturing processes and the demands of a global market-place.

To find out more about some of the latest ideas in textiles technology go to:
www.softswitch.co.uk
www.philips.com
www.symcad.com
http://levis-icd.com

Does Fashion have a Future?

Fashion fuels the textile and fibre industries which taint the air, poison water and use vast amounts of natural resources. It seems that environmental concerns are not a mere passing fad and that people will continue to demand that industries make changes for the better to industrial processes. Major designers such as Katharine Hamnett have already taken green ideas on board and some small companies, which specialised in garments made from reusable textiles, such as Scrap Scrap, have emerged.

Some fashion designers believe that fashion will go back to evolving more slowly rather than maintain the frantic rush of two or more collections per year. Meanwhile others continue to respond to the commercial pressures of grabbing as much publicity as they can from outrageous cat-walk shows. Their garments may sometimes look absurd and be quite inappropriate for everyday high-street wear, but they help maximise the media exposure of the name of the designer. In turn this helps sell perfume and fashion accessories which carry the designer's name – a highly lucrative market.

■ ACTIVITY

Carry out an investigation to find out people's attitudes towards fashion. You could explore one or more of the following:

▶ Does the concept of changing fashion contradict green philosophies?
▶ The need to ornament ourselves is older than the clothing industry. Why do you think we need to do this?
▶ Do designers create needs for us or do they respond to our demands?
▶ Why do we design, produce and buy things that we do not need?

Industry in the UK

The part of industry which manufactures textile products including clothing and footwear is **labour intensive** because it is still relatively dependent on a skilled work-force. It has been slower to utilise modern technologies than other industries. This is because the industry needs to remain flexible as styles change frequently.

The clothing industry has shrunk considerably over the past ten years because it is unable to compete with countries where labour is much cheaper and which can therefore produce products at much lower prices.

The part of the industry which manufactures the fabrics out of which textile products are made is more **capital intensive**. This means that investment in modern technology, such as CAD and CAM, is more worthwhile because this part of the industry is not so hard hit by competition from countries where labour is cheaper.

Absolutely Fabulous!

Computer technology will continue to bring changes in retailing as well as manufacture. It is already possible to buy a pair of custom-made jeans. This means that a customer can be measured in the shop, their measurements fed into a computer which facilitates the manufacture of a pair of jeans which are an exact fit for that individual customer.

Using CAD customers may be able to become more involved in the actual design of their own clothing, choosing colours and styles to suit them rather than settling for fashions which do not suit them.

The Global Economy

World textile and clothing markets account for a significant part of world trade and have seen faster growth in the last decade than many other industrial sectors. Production has moved eastwards towards the newly industrialised countries and many European retailers are investing in foreign sub-contractors to lower costs at home. Each year the industry becomes more global.

While most of the production growth is taking place in developing countries, the major consumer markets are in the USA, Western Europe and Japan. However, clothing and textile trade within Asia is growing steadily as people become more prosperous and can therefore afford more consumer items.

In Asia the clothing industry is growing much more quickly than the textile industry. This is because it can afford cheap labour but not new technology. Textile producers world-wide are finding that acquiring the latest technology is no longer an option. Less industrialised countries cannot afford to do this so it makes more sense for them to expand their clothing industries.

Presenting to the Client (1): in Perspective

For an interior design presentation a client needs to get a sense of what a design will look like when placed into the space it will be used in. There are various ways of doing this, such as a photo-collage, a computer-generated image or a three-dimensional model. Preparing a coloured perspective drawing is another widely used method.

Perspective

The word **perspective** comes from the Latin word *perspecta* meaning to look through.

Originally artists looked through windows at objects and noticed that if they drew what they saw onto the glass in front of them, the resulting picture looked very realistic, a two-dimensional representation of the three-dimensional object.

A perspective drawing recreates the illusion of objects getting smaller as they go into the distance and of parallel lines meeting on the horizon line. This is how we see objects and their surroundings in real life.

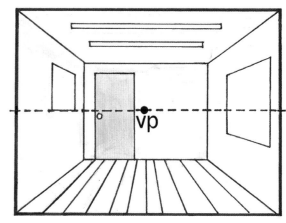

Look around yourself. If you have a tiled ceiling or floor, try to look from one end of the room to the other. What do you notice about the parallel lines of the tiles?

One-point perspective
If you think of the parallel lines of a railway track, they appear to meet in the distance. This is called the **vanishing point** and it appears on the horizon line. The horizon line appears at the height of the viewers eye and is also known as the eye level.

If you pick up a small object e.g. a pencil tin, and place it at eye level, directly in front of you (centrally) what do you see? If you move the object above eye level, you will see underneath the object, and below eye level, you will see above the object. What happens if you move the object to the left and right? How many surfaces can you see?

What you can see when the object is directly in front of you, on, above and below the eye level, can be drawn using one-point perspective.

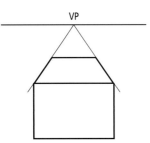

Two-point perspective
A two-point perspective drawing follows the same principles as a one-point perspective drawing except you have two vanishing points on the horizon line. You also begin your drawing with the corner edge of the object you wish to illustrate e.g. a cube.

This is an excellent way of illustrating an object or a view in a room.

It is a good idea to include a person in any interior perspective view. This helps give the space a sense of proportion, and shows you have taken the user into account in your design.

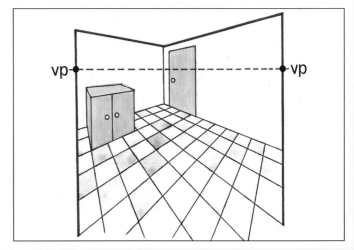

■ **ACTIVITY**

Can you draw a view of your cabin interior using one or two point perspective?

▷ Draw an outline of the cabin 4 x 2.5 m. (choose a scale that will fit your page). Mark every 0.5 m. Put in eye level at 1.5 m (average adult).

▷ Put your vanishing point (VP) centrally and draw faint construction lines from your vanishing point to each corner.

▷ Draw in the back wall of your cabin (about 1.5 m on the side scale).

▷ Marking the 0.5 m scale at the base of your picture plane, draw faint construction lines from the vanishing point to these marks. Draw a diagonal line from the back to front corner. Where this crosses your construction lines, draw in horizontal lines. This floor grid marks out every 0.5 m square and helps you place your furniture. The room is 4 m deep.

Once you have drawn your cabin design in perspective, trace it off using layout paper and render the drawing. Try to add light, shade, texture and pattern.

Draw one cabin interior in daylight and one in artificial light (evening).

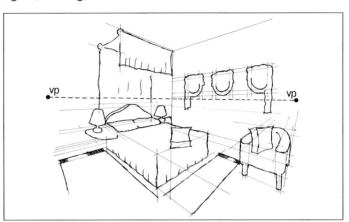

Presenting to the Client (2)

A SEA CRUISE

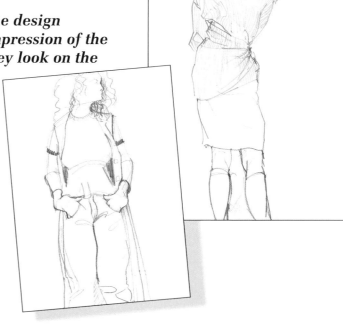

Successful fashion illustrations need to:

▷ **convey the spirit of the design**
▷ **give an immediate impression of the garments and how they look on the body**
▷ **contain all the information needed for the production of the garment.**

■ ACTIVITY

It is not easy to draw a figure that looks lively and as if the clothes really belong to it. Practise drawing a friend in various poses paying special attention to how the fabric of their clothes creases and drapes. Spend approximately five minutes on each pose and take turns at modelling until you have a collection of different poses to work from.

Alternatively draw poses from fashion magazines or books. Try to make these drawings look three dimensional by studying how the fabric hangs around the body.

Materials

Illustrators through history have used every method from wood block to collage to create beautiful **fashion illustrations**. Practise with different materials creating the right texture for the fabrics you have chosen and the correct mood for your theme.

The choice of paper is essential to the final look of the drawing. A heavy rough paper will give a 'natural', soft look. A smooth, shiny paper will look more 'slick'. Don't forget to stretch the paper when using water-based paints, pencils or inks.

You do not need to draw every part of the figure/clothes in detail. It is possible to use large strokes of colour to give the general shape. Details can be drawn on top or as a resist (e.g. wax crayon) in important areas.

Shading and the contrast of dark and light are essential to creating a three dimensional illusion and to bringing it to life.

In the Background

The background to your illustration can contrast to make the figure 'jump out' or harmonise.

▷ It could be a simple colour wash.
▷ You could cut your figure out and glue it onto a photograph or pattern.
▷ The figure could be drawn inside an interior.

The background could be an abstract drawing based upon the design theme e.g. pyramids.

Try sketching different compositions to see how they change the look of your illustration.

This illustration shows rough wool tartans, fake fur and knitted fabrics used in womenswear. Heavy watercolour paper has been used to get a rough texture. The blocks of colour have been created with watercolour paint and coloured pencils have been used to imitate the detailed tartan fabrics. The watercolour paper allows a wash of 'scotch mist' to be applied as a background from which the bright clothes stand out.

Presentation

Once you have completed your illustration you must think about how you will present it to the client. Your final **presentation boards** should include all the information a manufacturer would need to make the finished garment. The illustrations should 'sell' the idea to the client but you will need to use other methods to communicate the finer details of your design.

Annotations

Give your project a smart title. On your presentation boards include:

▶ the name of the client
▶ the name of the project
▶ any evocative words that will convey the mood of the project
▶ your name

and other relevant information such as:

▶ fabric content
▶ washing instructions
▶ costing breakdown
▶ design details e.g. position of invisible zips
▶ production details

Will you type or handwrite your annotations?

Working drawings

These are flat line drawings to scale. They are used in industry to give accurate information about proportion, exact placement of seams and fastenings. Usually only the back and front are drawn but you can include close ups of design features.

Fabric samples

Inclusion of fabric samples is essential to give the whole picture of a design. Try to present them neatly but do not glue down the whole sample as the client may want to feel the fabric not just look at it. Any patterns/prints should be shown with a full repeat if possible.

Mounting your Work

Composition

When mounting your work take some time to consider where to place working drawings, fabric samples etc. Try not to squash everything on to a page so that it is confusing but do think about overlapping.

Size

Size is important. Your work should be easy to handle and transport. How many boards will you use?

Materials

Think about this in the same way as when you chose a background for your illustration. The material you choose to mount your work on should contrast or harmonise with your work. The colour and texture of the material you use for mounting adds to the overall mood of your presentation.

Think of all the different types of materials you could mount your work on and consider their good and bad points. Experiment with materials such as thin sheet metal, wood, plastic, fabric, tracing paper, corrugated card, etc.

Stick your work onto the board.

PIERROT

■ ACTIVITY

Look at the work of artists who have used the clothed figure as a subject. Study historical fashion illustrations. How do drawings of the early twentieth century differ from modern illustrations?

Choose a favourite work of art and a fashion illustration and consider what makes them successful. Look at:

▶ composition
▶ pose
▶ colour
▶ texture
▶ style
▶ atmosphere
▶ materials.

Computer-aided Design (CAD)

You may already have developed some of your designs on computer. Check that they do not look too two dimensional and that they successfully convey the texture and nature of the fabric. CAD is especially useful for creating neat, accurate working drawings which can be changed very quickly.

A SEA CRUISE

realisation

Presenting to the Client (3)

On the Catwalk

Catwalk shows have always been popular with fashion designers. They are a very direct way of selling the finished design to a client and they are entertaining.

As with fashion illustration every part of a catwalk show should reflect the mood and style of the designs, be easy to understand and look professional.

A Virtual Prototype

A **virtual prototype** is a very high quality computer-generated image of a product, viewed on screen or printed out, which provides a photo-realistic impression of what the product will look like when made. These are used to help communicate a design idea to the client in a convincing way.

A virtual reality catwalk

When creating a **catwalk show** designers need to plan carefully the:
- ▶ music
- ▶ lighting
- ▶ decoration of venue/catwalk
- ▶ models – hair, make-up and accessories
- ▶ programme
- ▶ seating arrangements
- ▶ publicity and promotion
- ▶ cost.

KEY POINTS

- Don't forget that your illustrations and presentation are meant to sell your ideas to the client. They should be lively and exciting but very polished, i.e. professional.
- Give yourself time to practise at every stage. It would be a shame to ruin all your hard work by rushing your presentation stage.

IN YOUR PROJECT

- ▶ Which is the most appropriate way of presenting your work to a large audience or one client?
- ▶ Will you be displaying your work on a wall, desk, photographing or videoing it?

A Report

A formal **report** can be a good way of providing the client with information that can be taken away and studied later. It might include detailed information which covers things like:

- ▶ market research findings
- ▶ fashion trends
- ▶ developments in fibre technology
- ▶ the results of fabric tests
- ▶ an assessment of the environmental impact of the product

- ▶ costings
- ▶ proposals for manufacturing and production processes, including quality control and safety procedures.

The report will need to be typed up (or word-processed) and bound. Don't forget to include technical illustrations such as graphs, charts and diagrams.

Final Testing and Evaluation

A SEA CRUISE

A good way of assessing the success of your design solution is to do a presentation and ask your audience to take the part of clients and customers.

You will need to be prepared to justify your ideas and to discuss the pathway you have followed in arriving at your design solution.

Testing the Final Presentation

You could also assess how well people have understood your design proposals from your models, drawings and presentation work. For example you might ask them:

▷ what sort of people is the design aimed at?
▷ what words would you use to describe its colours, textures and shapes?
▷ what are the particular design features which make it distinctive?
▷ what does the logo say or suggest?

On behalf of Luxor Travel I would like to thank you for the excellent job you have made of developing the designs for our new cruise liner. I am pleased to enclose a complimentary ticket for the maiden voyage of the *Gift Of The Nile*.

Bon voyage!

INVITATION

GIFT OF THE
NILE
MAIDEN VOYAGE
ADMIT ONE + GUEST
PRESENT TO PURSER ON BOARDING

Final Evaluation

In your **evaluation** describe the tests you have carried out on your final product and the presentation, perhaps recording the results in chart form. Discuss the quality of the product (including how well it meets the specification) and the processes you went through while designing it.

In particular refer to how your final design needed to change to take account of the demands of mass-production.

Try to give a balanced evaluation weighing up the strengths against the weaknesses of your work, and your design.

If you had more time to develop your design further what would you do? How could you alter your product to make it simpler, quicker, cheaper and more efficient to manufacture?

Examination Questions

You should spend about one and a half hours answering the following questions. To complete the paper you will need some plain A4 and A3 paper, basic drawing equipment, and colouring materials. You are reminded of the need for good English and clear presentation in your answers.

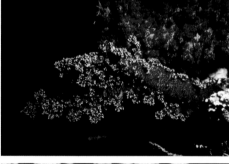

Before attempting the following questions you will need to do some preliminary research into:

● images and colours associated with underwater life
● how colour and pattern can be used in clothing and living spaces to create different effects.

Design Brief

You have been asked to design for one of the following clients:

1. A paint manufacturer who has developed a new range of colours
   based on inspiration from underwater life. A co-ordinating range of home furnishing products is to be produced to promote the paint colours. The furnishing products will be sold in DIY outlets throughout the country.
2. A major supermarket which wants to develop a co-ordinating range of fun clothing and accessories for boys and girls between the ages of five and ten. The products will be sold in their stores throughout the country.

In addition to the points above the specification for the products states that:

● the fabric is to be printed with images based on the theme of underwater life.
● they must be suitable for bulk manufacture.

You must choose either 1. or 2. and then relate all your answers to the following questions to the product range you have selected.

1. This question is about research for your product range. *(Total 11 marks).* See pages 78, 88-89

(a) Write down three ways in which you could find out the sort of products which would sell. *(3 marks)*

(b) Describe two ways in which you could use inspiration from underwater life in your designs for the products. *(4 marks)*

(c) Your products are aimed at a target market. Explain two ways in which the intended selling price might affect your designs. *(4 marks)*

2. This question is about the design of your product range. *(Total 39 marks)*. See pages 100-103, 118-119

(a) (i) Sketch initial ideas for two different products using the specification given. One of these ideas is to be developed into a final design. *(6 marks)*

(ii) Choose one of your ideas for development and explain why you have chosen this design. *(2 marks)*

(iii) Look carefully at the design you have chosen for development. Explain with reasons two things that will need to be modified to make the product easier to mass produce. *(4 marks)*

(b) Using sketches, labelling and notes, present a final design for your product. Show how you intend to use the theme of underwater life in your product.

Marks will be awarded for:

- choice of fabrics and components *(5 marks)*
- originality and inventiveness of the design *(3 marks)*
- use of colour *(2 marks)*
- form, function and quality of the design *(10 marks)*

(c) The products will be available in a range of colourways.

(i) What factors will affect the number of colourways to be made? *(3 marks)*

(ii) Explain how CAD can help with the development of the different colour ranges. *(4 marks)*

3. This question is about the fabric and the fabric decoration. *(Total 25 marks)*. See pages 90-93, 96-99, 126-127, 131

(a) The fabric is to be printed with images associated with underwater life.

(i) Name and evaluate the suitability of two different methods which could be used in the mass manufacture of the product. *(6 marks)*

(ii) Your client is anxious that the fabrics and method of decoration used for the products should be safe and environmentally friendly. Discuss the ways in which you could ensure this. *(6 marks)*

(iii) Discuss the advantages and disadvantages of the fabric being printed in another country before being made into products in the UK. *(6 marks)*

(b) Many fabrics used for fashion and furnishing products are blends. Name an appropriate blend of fibres for your product and explain why you consider it to be suitable. *(7 marks)*

4. This question is about the manufacture of the product you have designed. *(Total 21 marks)*. See pages 104-117, 120-125

(a) A production plan will be needed before the manufacture of your product begins.

(i) Why will this need to be worked out carefully? *(3 marks)*

(ii) Explain the difference between main and sub-assembly lines in the production system. *(4 marks)*

(iii) Draw up a production chart to show the main and sub-assembly lines that would be needed when making your product in quantity. *(6 marks)*

(b) A factory quality control system sets tolerance levels for the manufacture of products.

(i) What are tolerance levels? *(2 marks)*

(ii) Describe tolerance levels that might be set for the manufacture of two different parts of your product. Explain why it is important that these parts are made to the agreed tolerances. *(6 marks)*

5. This question is about consumer issues related to the products. *(Total 9 marks)*. See page 72

(a) Give three reasons why your product will need to be packaged before going into the shops. *(3 marks)*

(b) A consumer has bought one of your products and has changed his/her mind about the colour and taken it back to the shop for a refund.

(i) What are his/her rights in this situation? *(3 marks)*

(ii) What would his/her rights be if the item were faulty? *(3 marks)*

Total marks = 105

Textiles Today: Museum Exhibition

Your local museum is putting on an exhibition called Celebrating Textiles Today. *It wishes to display different fabrics and fabric combinations in an imaginative and creative way. You are asked to design a decorative title banner which is to be hung in the main entrance gallery. You will need to show how it would look in the gallery.*

Embellishing Fabrics (pages 40 and 42)

Presenting to the Client (pages 140 to 145)

Investigation

Go to a local museum and have a look at the type of exhibition that is on display.

▷ Where are any textiles used?
▷ How are they used? Do they have a practical use, i.e. carry text, or are they purely aesthetic?
▷ If there are no textiles present, where could they be used to give information or add drama?
▷ What fabric gifts are available for purchase?

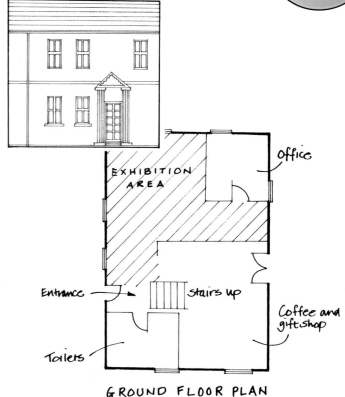

GROUND FLOOR PLAN

Design Specification

The actual banner will measure 200 cm (2 metres) high by 75 cm wide. Your banner may need to be made to scale in order to complete the task on time. At a scale of 1:5 (i.e. five times smaller than actual size), the banner you make would be 40 cm by 15 cm. Alternatively you could just make a part of it (e.g. 30 cm by 30 cm) full size

The banner can have cut outs, images and text. It might reflect one of the following themes:

▷ the sea
▷ medieval England
▷ recycled materials
▷ the jungle.

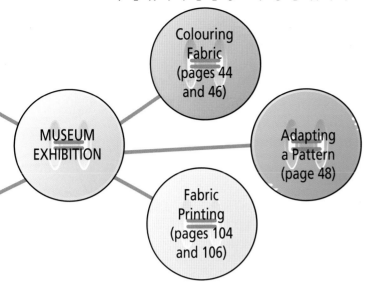

MUSEUM EXHIBITION

Colouring Fabric (pages 44 and 46)

Adapting a Pattern (page 48)

Fabric Printing (pages 104 and 106)

First Thoughts

You may wish to start your project with a collage made up of relevant research materials. These materials could include related objects, illustrations, photocopies, magazine cut-outs, etc.

Next think about alternative designs and colour themes. Remember your banner will be hanging from the ceiling and will be seen from a distance. Therefore it must be dramatic, with detailing which is not too small to lose its effect.

Be bold and adventurous. You could also appliqué all sorts of unusual objects which might not be made of fabric, but which would enhance the overall effect. What sort of objects can you think of?

Developing the Details

Use annotated sketches to show the effects you want to create. Think about colour, texture, pattern and shape, as well as possibilities for embellishment. Include drawings which will show your design full-size in its setting.

You should do some experiments to test out your ideas on samples or scraps of fabric.

▷ Which fabric has the best weight and hangs true?
▷ Is the fabric strong enough for any appliqué work?
▷ How well does it take any dyes?

Planning the Making

Decide exactly what you will need to make to present your idea. Ideally you should aim to make a full size banner, but if this is not possible decide if you are going to make a small section full-size or a complete small-scale version. If so you will need to also prepare either

▷ a neat perspective drawing to show what the full-size banner would look like in place
▷ a scale model to put your small-scale version into.

Estimate how long the various stages of making will take. Which operations will be done by hand and which by machine? Do you have all the materials and tools you need?

Final Testing and Evaluation

Could other people identify the theme you chose?

Could they easily read any lettering?

What other comments did they make about the colours, patterns and textures you used?

Do you agree with the things they said?

Did you do enough research?

What did you learn from your tests on fabric weight and strengths of fibres? How did this influence your fnal design?

Did the making go according to plan? If not how could you improve it next time?

Teenage Garments and Accessories

Project Suggestions

As a designer you have been asked to produce some designs as suitable for sale in a chain of boutiques which specialise in beachwear and accessories.

Designing for a Market (page 59)

Colouring Fabric (page 44)

Designing for Manufacture (pages 116 and 118)

Investigation

List different types of beachwear and accessories.

▷ What is fashionable at the moment? Are bright colours, dark/neutral colours or printed textiles popular? Collect some visual material to complement your research.

▷ Carry out a survey among friends and family to find out about their likes and dislikes in this area and any important practical points.

▷ Research into existing products on the market. Disassemble some relevant garments and accessories paying particular attention to design, fabrics used and construction.

Specification

Remember to write a detailed specification.

Specification

✔ I am going to design and make a sarong.
✔ It will be for women aged 16 upwards.
✔ It must not cost more than...
✔ It could be worn during the evenings as well.
✔ The material will need to be...
✔ I am going to design and print the fabric myself.

First Thoughts

Quickly sketch some ideas for the shape and style of your garment/accessory. You will also need to develop some initial ideas for themes for the print

Dip dyed cotton or silk with screen printed palm tree design

Tie and dye sunburst

Batik sun and sea design

Appliqué fish and seaweed. Embroidered scales and bubbles.

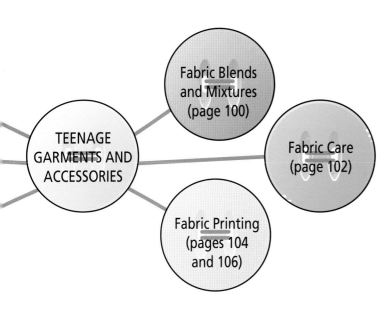

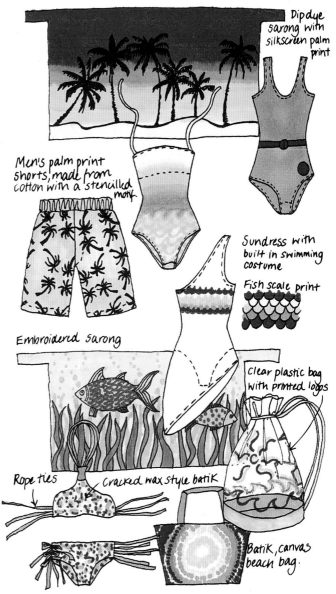

Dip dye sarong with silkscreen palm print

Men's palm print shorts, made from cotton with a stencilled motif.

Sundress with built in swimming costume

Fish scale print

Embroidered sarong

Clear plastic bag with printed logos

Rope ties

Cracked wax style batik

Batik, canvas beach bag.

Developing the Final Idea

Develop one idea
in greater depth. In particular think about:

▷ style
▷ material
▷ decorative techniques
▷ finishing and fastenings.

Test Pieces

Make a small sample using the technique and material
that you intend to use.

▷ Is it effective?
▷ Is the technique right for the fabric?
▷ Did it take you a long time?
▷ Do you need to make any
  alterations to your design?

Plan the Making

Identify the different processes
of printing, cutting out,
construction and finishing
you will need to cover.

▷ What tools and
  materials will
  you need?
▷ What needs to be prepared
  in advance?
▷ How will you check the
  quality of making?

Final Testing

Present your final realisation to someone from your
target market.

▷ How did they react?
▷ Did they enjoy trying it on?
▷ Would they wear it?

Final Evaluation

Discuss the process of designing and making you used as
well as the success of your final design.

▷ Refer to the comments made during testing. Do you
  agree with what was said?
▷ If you had more time how would you develop your
  idea further?
▷ How could such a garment be produced in quantity?

Index